ENGLISH LANGUAGE
LEARNERS
IN THE
MATHEMATICS
CLASSROOM

ENGLISH LANGUAGE LEARNERS
IN THE
MATHEMATICS
CLASSROOM

Debra Coggins
Drew Kravin
Grace Dávila Coates
Maria Dreux Carroll

Foreword by
Miriam Leiva

CORWIN PRESS
A SAGE Publications Company
Thousand Oaks, CA 91320

For information:

 Corwin Press
A Sage Publications Company
2455 Teller Road
Thousand Oaks, California 91320
www.corwinpress.com

Sage Publications Ltd.
1 Oliver's Yard
55 City Road
London EC1Y 1SP
United Kingdom

Sage Publications India Pvt. Ltd.
B-42, Panchsheel Enclave
Post Box 4109
New Delhi 110 017 India

Printed in the United States of America

Library of Congress Cataloging-in-Publication Data

English language learners in the mathematics classroom / Debra Coggins . . . [et al.].
    p. cm.
Includes bibliographical references and index.
ISBN 978-1-4129-3759-7 (cloth)
ISBN 978-1-4129-3760-3 (pbk.)

 1. Mathematics—Study and teaching—United States. 2. English language—Study and teaching—Foreign speakers—Activity programs. I. Coggins, Debra. II. Title.

QA13.E48 2007
510.71—dc22

                                          2006034596

This book is printed on acid-free paper.

11 12 13 14 15 10 9 8 7 6 5

Acquiring Editor:	Jean Ward
Editorial Assistant:	Jordan Barbakow
Production Editor:	Denise Santoyo
Typesetter:	C&M Digitals (P) Ltd.
Indexer:	Kathy Paparchontis
Cover Designer:	Rose Storey
Graphic Designer:	Karine Hovsepian
Illustrator:	Celia P. Stevenson

Contents

Preface   ix

Foreword   xiii
    Miriam A. Leiva

About the Authors   xv

Chapter 1. **Developing Conversational Language: Help English
    Learners Talk-to-Learn During Mathematics Lessons**   **1**

Rationale From Research   1
Mathematics Teaching Example   2
    Geometric Attributes   2
Discussion of the Mathematics Teaching Example   6
    Mathematics Goals   6
    Language Goals   6
    Students of Varying Language Proficiency Levels
       Working Together   7
    Talking and Doing Help With Thinking   7
    Developing Awareness of Attributes of Geometric Shapes   8
Teaching Tips   8
Discussion of Conversational Language   9
    Why is conversational language important in
       learning mathematics?   10
    Why is a problem-solving approach to mathematics
       helpful to English learners' language development?   10
    What are characteristics of effective prompts for stimulating
       conversational language?   11
    How can you ensure that all children will have a chance
       to speak and to ask questions?   11
Conversational Language Research   12
Practice and Discussion Questions   14

Chapter 2. **Developing Academic Language: Develop Mathematics
    Concepts and Vocabulary for English Learners**   **15**

Rationale From Research   15
Mathematics Teaching Example   16
    Word Problems   16
Discussion of the Mathematics Teaching Example   20
    Mathematics Goals   20

Language Goals 21

Support Through Primary Language and Cognates 21

Developing Specific Math Vocabulary 21

Opportunities to Use Academic Language 22

Teaching Decisions 22

Teaching Tips 23

Discussion of Academic Language Development 25

Why is it usually not productive to go over new key
vocabulary at the beginning of a math lesson? 25

Why is it suggested that we not emphasize key words
in math problems? 26

Why do we need to differentiate discussion goals
for levels of English language development? 26

Academic Language Research 27

Practice and Discussion Questions 28

Chapter 3. **Scaffolding: Give Support for Both
Mathematics and Language Learning** **29**

Rationale From Research 29

Mathematics Teaching Example 30

Algebraic Reasoning 30

Discussion of the Mathematics Teaching Example 34

Mathematics Goals 34

Language Goals 34

Advance Organizers 34

Creating Access to the Lesson 35

Creating Support During the Lesson 35

Teaching Tips 35

Discussion of Scaffolding in Mathematics 36

How does cooperative group work provide scaffolding? 37

What are benefits of emphasizing problem
solving in mathematics lessons for English learners? 38

How is scaffolding of new mathematics concepts different
from carefully planned direct instruction? 38

How is scaffolding used to support English
language development during mathematics lessons? 39

Scaffolding Research 39

Practice and Discussion Questions 40

Chapter 4. **The Role of Concrete Materials: Utilize Objects
to Develop Mathematical Understanding for English Learners** **41**

Rationale From Research 41

Mathematics Teaching Example 42

District Fifth-Grade Benchmark 42

Discussion of the Mathematics Teaching Example 46

Mathematics Goals 46

Language Goals 47

Building Understanding by Using Concrete Materials 47

Expanding Understanding Through Multiple Representations 47

Preplanning Key Lessons 48

Teaching Tips | 48
Discussion of Concrete Materials in Mathematics | 49
    When is it appropriate to use concrete materials in the
       mathematics classroom? | 50
    What should teachers be aware of when using
       concrete materials? | 51
    Is the concrete-pictorial-abstract sequence still promoted? | 51
Concrete Materials Research | 52
Practice and Discussion Questions | 53

**Chapter 5. Visual Learning: Provide Mathematical and
Organizational Representations as a Regular Component
of Instruction** | **55**

Rationale From Research | 55
Mathematics Teaching Example | 56
    Two-Digit Multiplication | 56
Discussion of the Mathematics Teaching Example | 65
    Mathematics Goals | 65
    Language Goals | 65
    Use of an Advance Organizer | 66
    Visual Learning Strategies, Cognitive Tasks,
       and Language Development | 66
Teaching Tips | 67
Discussion of Visual Learning in Mathematics | 68
    What are graphic organizers, advance organizers,
       and diagrams, and why are they important? | 68
    Are all learners visual learners? | 70
Visual Learning Research | 71
Practice and Discussion Questions | 72

**Chapter 6. Questioning Strategies: Ask Questions to Foster
Students' Learning of Mathematics and English** | **73**

Rationale From Research | 73
Mathematics Teaching Example | 74
    Probability Introduction | 74
Discussion of the Mathematics Teaching Example | 79
    Mathematics Goals | 79
    Language Goals | 79
    Multiple Goals When Asking Questions | 80
    Questions and Discussions Between Students | 80
Teaching Tips | 80
Discussion of Questioning Strategies in Mathematics | 81
    How does placing a focus on questioning affect English
       learners and their teachers? | 82
    Should the levels of questions we ask students change as
       their levels of fluency increase? | 83
    How can we ensure that we are challenging our students
       through our questioning? | 83
    What are levels of questioning that can elicit verbal responses
       from students with various levels of English acquisition? | 84

Questioning in Mathematics Research 86

Practice and Discussion Questions 87

Chapter 7. **Comprehensible Input: Combine Many Strategies to Develop Mathematics Concepts Through Clear and Effective Instruction** **89**

Rationale From Research 89

Mathematics Teaching Example 90

    Perimeter and Multiplicative Scaling 90

Discussion of the Mathematics Teaching Example 95

    Mathematics Goals 95

    Language Goals 96

    Teaching Decisions 96

    Continuously Creating Access 96

    Successfully Getting Started 97

    Using Strategies to Provide Comprehensible Input 97

Teaching Tips 98

Discussion of Comprehensible Input in Mathematics 99

    How can we maximize students' comprehension of a mathematics lesson? 100

    How is comprehensible input incorporated in the teaching of mathematics concepts? 100

    What is the role of constant monitoring in English learners' mathematics classes? 101

    What is the role of thinking and learning strategies in English learners' mathematics classes? 101

Comprehensible Input Research 102

Practice and Discussion Questions 102

Appendix **105**

Exhibit A1.1 Geometric Shapes 106

Exhibit A3.1 Blank Planning Map for Effective EL Mathematics Lessons 107

Exhibit A3.2 Lesson-Planning Map: Example From Chapter 3— Planning Map for Effective EL Mathematics Lessons 109

Exhibit A6.1 Snail Races: Instructions and Game Board 111–112

Exhibit A6.2 Sample Questions to Support All Learners and Develop Mathematical Thinking 113

References **115**

Index **121**

Preface

Fundamentally, this book proposes that if we teach mathematics by following commonly accepted "best practices," we may actually overlook English learners, because they have very specific needs. On the other hand, if we teach mathematics in ways that benefit English learners, then all students will benefit from the rich repertoire of strategies designed to create access to mathematics content. In *English Language Learners in the Mathematics Classroom,* we journey through a short list of specific, research-based strategies proven to be helpful to English learners. It is not enough to simply provide general suggestions such as "increase students' opportunities to make sense of mathematics and to speak and listen in class." We discuss each learning strategy through a specific mathematics problem and classroom scenario, with the teaching examples addressing mathematics topics of importance across Grades 1 through 7 and beyond. Through discussion of instruction of specific mathematics content, we demonstrate our belief in purposefully planning and delivering instruction that combines rigorous mathematics content with attention to language development and learning strategies.

While there are various types of support programs for English learners, covering them all is beyond the scope of this book. (The reader may wish to refer online to Valdez, Svedkauskaite, and McNabb, 2002, for an overview of types of instructional programs for Limited English Proficient Students.) In general, when students have not already learned targeted mathematics concepts and skills in their primary language, it is most effective to use primary language for initial instruction (Garrison & Mora, 2005). Currently, many teachers are not able to provide primary language instruction to all of their students, and in fact they teach students of varying levels of fluency with whom they do not share the primary language. Therefore, in this book we focus on teaching mathematics and providing for English language development in general settings. Still, when possible, teachers should take advantage of any opportunity to provide primary language support as a general strategy for providing access to mathematics content and improving language development.

Although much attention has been given to the importance of building on students' prior knowledge as a way to move into new learning, we remind the reader that for English learners, establishing prior knowledge includes identifying cultural connections as well as acknowledging and affirming the mathematics experiences and knowledge brought to the classroom. Capitalizing on these experiences helps English learners make connections between what they already know and what they are now learning.

Learning in both formal and informal contexts involves language and communication. Therefore Chapter 1 is titled "Developing Conversational Language." When a teacher provides frequent opportunities to listen to and speak about mathematics, English learners have many opportunities to gain access to the instructional content and also to improve conversational language skills. The teaching example of sorting shapes in Chapter 1 demonstrates how a focus on communication supports students in making sense of new topics while at the same time providing opportunities to practice listening to and speaking English. Conversational, everyday language bridges the development of mathematics concepts and offers links to accompanying academic vocabulary. Conversational language skills are extended as the teacher models the use of targeted phrases, words, and questions. The mathematical tasks and student grouping structures that are selected act as catalysts for students' frequent use of English.

From conversational language, we continue in Chapter 2 with "Developing Academic Language." Readers are made aware of the challenge in teaching students who must develop new academic language while learning new mathematics concepts. The main focus is on students' development of vocabulary that is specific to the learning of mathematics in the context of lessons on important mathematics concepts and skills. Techniques that are different from teaching new vocabulary in a reading lesson are discussed. The teaching example illustrates instruction related to word problems involving *more, less,* and *fewer* comparisons. The lesson demonstrates purposeful concept and academic language development.

While language development is crucial to providing access for English learners, instruction must be made accessible through specific techniques and strategies. Thus, Chapter 3 focuses on "Scaffolding"—systematic ways teachers can create pathways for English learners to understand and learn the content of the lessons that are presented. This chapter gives greatest emphasis to scaffolding mathematics concept development, but it also gives suggestions for scaffolding language development. Various forms of support for English learners are discussed. The mathematics content of algebraic thinking is used as the vehicle to discuss scaffolding, with an example of using an engaging problem as the focus during an initial introduction to linear functions.

Chapter 4 covers "The Role of Concrete Materials" because this type of active learning is helpful both for English learners in all subjects and for all learners of mathematics. The main focus of this chapter is the importance of active learning, with a focus on sense making, particularly with the use of tangible objects, including manipulative materials. The Chapter 4 teaching example has a sample mathematics districtwide benchmark assessment item as a starting point for the discussion of concrete materials support for English learners. Simple plastic discs are used to help students learn about multiplying fractions and related concepts and skills—demonstrating that "manipulatives" do not need to be unusual or complex, nor are they only for young students.

Closely connected to the use of concrete materials is the importance of "Visual Learning," the title of Chapter 5. Again, this strategy is key for English learners and is connected to the role of representations in mathematics. The area model of multiplication is examined through the lens of visual learning. Visual learning tools, including graphic organizers, mathematical diagrams, and advance organizers are explained and their importance emphasized. Not only are visual learning tools advocated for teacher use, but students can learn to use these tools as well.

Chapter 6 returns to an emphasis on both concept and language development with "Questioning Strategies." An introductory probability lesson is the context used to demonstrate the need for appropriate levels of questioning relative to students' language levels and also the need to probe all students' thinking in mathematics. The importance of the questions that a teacher asks and the problems that a teacher poses is discussed in terms of both students' opportunities to learn mathematics and opportunities to further develop language skills. Changes in a teacher's questioning practices have the potential to have a powerful effect on students' learning.

In Chapter 7, we bring all of the ideas examined in the book together under the heading "Comprehensible Input." This chapter serves as a conclusion because, ultimately, every strategy we have examined serves the main goal of instruction for English learners and indeed for all students—providing comprehensible input that facilitates learning of mathematics and language. Strategies for making instruction comprehensible include relating to prior life experience, using multiple modalities, making connections to other known mathematics, and identifying connections among representations. Relatively small shifts in lesson presentation may have a large positive effective on the learning of English learners. In the teaching example, a teacher uses several strategies to provide his students with access to a challenging problem-solving task that combines perimeter and multiplicative relationships such as "three times as long."

Each chapter, in addition to its dual focus on a specific strategy and a specific mathematics teaching example, has a common structure:

- The subject is introduced in relation to relevant research.
- A content-specific mathematics problem is presented.
- A lesson involving this content is described in the teaching example. (Here the chapters vary, as the lesson is portrayed through a variety of formats, including classroom scenarios, grade-level discussions and planning, and professional development assignments. Note that a lesson serves to illustrate the chapter topic but is not offered as a model lesson. Each lesson is expected to be a catalyst for conversation, reflection, and suggestions among teachers.)
- Commentary on the teaching example is given.
- Teaching tips are listed.
- Further discussion of the chapter topic is offered.
- Additional relevant research is summarized.
- Discussion questions are suggested.

All names used in the book have been fictionalized. Numerals such as 6 or 24 have purposely been used for ease of reading when specific quantities are an important part of following a lesson scenario or discussion. At times, numbers are purposely spelled out within dialogues to emphasize the verbal form that students hear or say.

In creating *English Language Learners in the Mathematics Classroom*, the four authors came together from different professional backgrounds. We brought different but overlapping expertise to tackle the problem of how to provide specific suggestions for teaching mathematics to English learners. By combining our individual backgrounds (in bilingual education, preservice teaching, mathematics education, elementary and middle school teaching, professional development work with teachers, school and classroom coaching, and theoretical foundations), we have broadened the research and experience base of what we could have done individually.

We hope that this book finds many varied uses as:

- Preservice course material
- Part of a professional development course or summer institute for classroom teachers
- A vehicle for site-based teacher collaboration
- Individual reading and reflection

Ultimately, this book is not intended to be a comprehensive treatment of all the work in the field of English language development and mathematics, but rather, it is intended to help teachers focus on a few key strategies with the potential of high impact. We look forward to additional contributions to this burgeoning field. By discussing several critical strategies we hope to demonstrate that even when a teacher does not speak the same primary language as his or her students, English learners can be supported in learning significant, challenging mathematics. In this way, mathematics becomes an exciting component of a positive future for English learners.

Foreword

Teachers in today's classrooms are looking at new faces that mirror the diverse population in our country. Whereas in the past educators focused on different learning styles, today we must deal with many other differences, such as culture, language, ethnicity, social and economic status of the family, as well as physiological and psychological differences. The population of students referred to as "English learners" exhibits all these differences within one group.

The premise of this book is *to tackle these differences through implementing research-based teaching strategies that work specifically for English learners* and, surprisingly, also benefit all students. If we employ the propositions in this volume in our classrooms, we will not only have new tools to help English learners, but we can open the doors to mathematics for other students as well, with the result of greater achievement by all.

English Language Learners in the Mathematics Classroom provides important and useful information supported by scholarly research and examples in the form of challenging yet reachable lessons along with details on each proposed strategy. When reviewing this book, it becomes clear that there are many audiences of teachers, preservice and inservice, who need to implement the ideas presented within.

This book is ideal for an inservice professional development program in a variety of ways: within a school, with teachers working in small groups by grade levels, discussing among groups vertically and horizontally, and planning for various levels of students' language proficiency; within a district, a professional development model of Read, Reflect, Discuss, Learn, Implement, and Report offers the advantage of creative grouping by various criteria such as grade level, language proficiency, level of mathematical fluency, and needs of individual schools.

As a mathematics teacher educator, I recognize this book as a helpful resource for preservice teachers as they *begin* their education program and classroom observations. The information here is necessary for all educators: those in graduate programs can further explore topics or chapters as they pursue their own action research and later as they develop major research papers that may lead to further research culminating in a thesis or dissertation.

What must we provide for our English learners in the mathematics classroom? The authors of *English Language Learners in the Mathematics Classroom* persuade us through a careful sequencing of chapters to develop conversational and academic language, to make the mathematics accessible through scaffolding for concept development, to encourage active learning or "doing" mathematics, and to use questioning strategies and creative groupings that promote communication and learning. All of these components lead to the appropriate development of mathematics for English learners: language, concepts and skills, and the confidence necessary to succeed.

—*Miriam A. Leiva*
Bonnie E. Cone Distinguished Professor for Teaching
Professor of Mathematics Emerita
The University of North Carolina
President, TODOS: Mathematics for All

About the Authors

Debra Coggins is a mathematics education consultant with experience advising districts, coaching teachers, and developing and delivering professional development. As a writer, she has helped develop a number of professional development programs for teachers of mathematics. These include creating CORE Math: Building Strong Foundations, assisting with the development of the Math Case Methods Project and Math Pathways and Pitfalls at WestEd, and coordinating the writing of America's Choice Core Assignments. She was the lead writer of *A Mathematics Source Book for Elementary and Middle School Teachers: Key Concepts, Teaching Tips, and Learning Pitfalls,* a resource book for teachers and professional developers. Coggins has presented at local, state, and national conferences and has a particular interest in strategies for supporting English learners and the use of diagrams when teaching concepts related to operations and proportional reasoning. She currently assists the Oakland Unified School District new small middle schools with teaching strategies for reaching English learners in mathematics classes, and has 17 years teaching experience in Grades K–12.

Drew Kravin is a mathematics coordinator for the Alameda County Office of Education (ACOE), where he codirects and teaches in several specialized professional development programs for teachers, K–12. Among his responsibilities, he serves as codirector of ACCLAIM, the Alameda County Collaborative for Learning and Instruction in Mathematics, a professional development program in partnership with California State University East Bay that has provided training for more than 2,500 teachers since 2000. He also serves as codirector of two California Mathematics and Science Partnership grants, whose purpose is to institutionalize mathematics coaching support in several districts. In addition, he is coordinator of the Student Work Profile, Internet-based software that facilitates teacher analysis of student work and that also includes a student online reasoning component. Kravin served as mathematics and assessment specialist at ACOE prior to his position as mathematics coordinator, was a visiting educator at the California Department of Education, and was a writer for state and national standards. He has had a long-standing involvement in bilingual development both personally and professionally, including its connections to mathematics, and he has been a classroom teacher primarily at the elementary level and a mathematics educator of Grades K–12 for more than 22 years.

Grace Dávila Coates is Director of FAMILY MATH, an international program dedicated to bringing families together for the purpose of investigating mathematical ideas, raising awareness of the role of mathematics in education, and opening doors to mathematics understanding and appreciation. FAMILY MATH is based at the Lawrence Hall of Science at the University of California, Berkeley. Grace is the primary author of *Family Math for Young Children* and *Family Math II: Achieving Success in Mathematics.* She has designed many professional development models used statewide, nationally, and internationally, focusing on the needs of English learners in mathematics. Coates has presented at local, state, and national conferences and has published numerous articles on mathematics education, English learners, family involvement, and language development. She has been a bilingual classroom teacher in Grades PreK–8 and a mathematics educator for 24 years.

Maria Dreux Carroll is Adjunct Professor at San Francisco State University and Holy Names University in Oakland, California, where she teaches preservice teachers mathematics methods. She recently retired from her position as mathematics specialist with the Alameda County Office of Education, but has continued to codirect the Regional Mathematics Peer Coaching Support Network. Carroll also worked as a mathematics specialist, coach, and classroom teacher with the Oakland Unified School District, where she created a mathematics coaching support program for 25 Title I schools. She became interested in the intersection of bilingual education, English language development (ELD), and mathematics. As a result, she began to develop special staff development presentations to address the needs of bilingual and English language learners. Maria has presented at local, state, and national conferences addressing the needs of teachers in mathematics content and pedagogy. Carroll has been a classroom teacher in Grades K–9 and a mathematics educator for more years than she wishes to count, including service in Washington, DC; Baltimore, Maryland; and Oakland, California.

1

Developing Conversational Language

*Help English Learners Talk-to-Learn
During Mathematics Lessons*

RATIONALE FROM RESEARCH ■

Conversational language plays an important role in the mathematics classroom. The term refers to nonacademic language and usually is the first type of language acquired by second language learners (Cummins, 2000). Conversational language is sometimes referred to as "everyday language," "natural language," or "social communication." It includes informal language that students might use with peers or adults while playing, shopping, and completing household tasks. According to Cummins (2000), these Basic Interpersonal Communication Skills (BICS) are less cognitively demanding and are often acquired in 1 or 2 years. Using conversational language involves more than knowing words and grammar. Knowledge of sociolinguistic aspects of a language and styles of discourse also aid in communication. For example, knowing how to use politeness features of a language, how to catch listeners' attention, and how to change topics during a conversation are all language skills that are useful both in and out of the classroom.

1

Green (2005) asserts that effective teachers "design learning activities to be challenging, engaging, relevant, and directed to student motivations; emphasize the process of learning and its excitement as a quest" (p. 43). Learning is a social endeavor. Mathematics lessons can be structured so that they entice students to stretch and use the new language to communicate, especially when engaging, cognitively demanding tasks are presented. Learning includes talking in informal ways about ideas and making connections to familiar experiences and ideas. Khisty (1995) describes the mathematics register as "a set of unique meanings and structures expressed through everyday language" (p. 282). Conversational language and development of the mathematics register serve as learning tools in the mathematics classroom, and mathematics lessons can lead to increased acquisition of English language skills.

The National Council of Teachers of Mathematics points out that conversational language makes it possible to teach children important formal mathematical terminology:

> Children need introductions to the language and conventions of mathematics, at the same time maintaining a connection to their informal knowledge and language. They should hear mathematical language being used in meaningful contexts. . . . Young children need to learn words for comparing and for indicating position and direction at the same time they are developing an understanding of counting and number words. (National Council of Teachers of Mathematics, 2000, p. 75)

Notice that in the following mathematics teaching example, students engage in informal conversation with peers while they learn about geometric attributes. In addition, students make use of their conversational language skills as they move toward learning academic language terms.

■ MATHEMATICS TEACHING EXAMPLE

Geometric Attributes

Sorting Shapes

Get Ready:
   Work in your Group of Four.

Do:

1. The Materials Person gets 8 or more cut-out shapes.

2. Talk about how you will sort the shapes into two groups.

3. Sort the shapes into two piles.

4. Explain your answer to this question: "Why do these belong together?"

5. Be ready to show your teacher your work and tell about it.

6. Start over and sort again with a different sorting rule.

Figure 1.1   Shapes to copy and cut out for sorting activities.

NOTE: See the Appendix for the full-sized figure.

Ms. Wilson, a second-grade teacher who has many English learners (ELs) in her class, has regularly had her students work and talk in small cooperative groups during their math hour. During the previous day's lesson, the students worked with the same set of geometric shapes. Each child got to pull a shape out of a bag and was asked to say, "My shape has . . ." in order to begin to build vocabulary to describe attributes of the shapes.

To begin this lesson, students are seated on a rug at the front of the room. Trays of shapes have been set out at each group's table.

MS. WILSON: I want you to think in your minds about the time we took a handful of objects from our box of "Treasures." We put them into piles and had reasons why they belonged in the different piles. Everyone, tell your neighbor what we called "putting into piles for a reason." What does it mean? . . . That's right, I heard people say, "sorting." [Ms. Wilson writes "sorting" on the board.] When we sort, we think about how some things are alike, why they belong together, and how the other things are different. That is our sorting rule.

MS. WILSON: So, today you see the shapes that we used yesterday in the tray at your tables. I want you to go to your tables and work with your group. Here are two paper sorting mats to hold your sorted piles. One person will take a turn getting at least eight shapes. Work together to put the shapes into two piles and have a reason why the shapes in each pile belong together. [Ms. Wilson holds up a rectangle and a parallelogram and gestures.] For example, should I put these shapes in the same pile or in different piles? I could do it either way. I just need to have a reason why they are alike or different, and to talk to my group about it. I'll let you work on it a while. When I come around, I'll ask you what your reason is for sorting the way you did. Then I'll push them together again. [She motions with her hands.] Then, you can figure out another way to put them into piles with reasons.

The students work in their groups for about 15 minutes while Ms. Wilson moves among the groups to clarify the instructions as needed and to ask questions. She leaves a tape recorder running at Table 3 to capture the students' spontaneous conversation:

LAURA (L):   I can do it. [She begins to take a few shapes to make a design, but looks over at other tables.]

DANIEL (D):   The teacher said we put these in piles.

ERNESTO (E):   I like this one [holds up a thin parallelogram]. Racing car. [He pushes it along the table.]

L: My car fast.

CAMILLE (C):   This one's pointy. [Holds up the isosceles triangle.]

E: This baseball. [Holds up circle.]

MS. WILSON (to the whole class):   Remember, you're sorting, putting the shapes into piles. So, talk at your tables about what you see, not what you could pretend. I heard someone say, "The circle is like a baseball," and that shows you have a good imagination. But, today we want to talk about how the shapes are alike and different. Think about what each shape feels like. When I hold this circle in my hand, how does it feel compared to this hexagon? Talk about it with your group.

E: It's sharp. [Holds the hexagon in one hand and the circle in the other hand.]

L: Goes like this. [Runs hand around the circle and rolls it carefully] The ball rolling.

D: It's not a ball; it's flat, it's smooth.

C: Let's put all the smooth ones over here. [Pushes the circle to one of the mats.] Ernesto, put the pointy one over there. [Points to the other mat.]

L: What's about this one? [Holds up the trapezoid.]

E: Sharp. [Touches finger to the tip of the trapezoid.] Blast off spaceship! [He moves it through the air.]

D: It's pointy, too.

L: [Holds the trapezoid in front of Ernesto.] Ernesto, put it with pointy ones.

E: I do it. [Moves the trapezoid to the mat with the triangle and the hexagon.]

C: [Picks up the equilateral triangle.] This is pointy, too. Let's put all the pointy ones here.

D: Let me get some. I'll get some more pointy shapes. [He takes some of the other polygons and puts them with the "pointy" shapes.]

E: I get rolly ones. [Picks up the curved shape and oval and puts them on the mat with the circle.]

L: Look, mine is like rolly one. [Puts the regular octagon on top of the circle.]

E: [Looks at Laura with puzzlement. Starts to take the octagon from Laura.]

D: No, put it in the other pile.

C: It's not a box, Laura! But it goes over there.

E: Pointy ones. [Puts the octagon with the polygons.]

L: What left?

E: Pointy. [Picks up the irregular hexagon and puts it with the polygons.]

C: That one is a box! [Points to the rhombus.]

        [Ms. Wilson comes over, seeing that they are just about finished with the sorting.]

Ms. Wilson: So, what have you got here?

E: Pointy ones here. [He points to the appropriate pile.]

C: We put the squares and triangles over here.

L: And round ones there.

Ms. Wilson: And what's the same about all these? How are they alike? [Points to the mat with polygons.]

Figure 1.2   One group of students' sorting work, with differing opinions on where to place the regular hexagon.

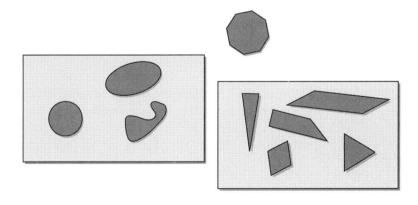

L:	All pointy. [Points to each of the corners of the triangles.]
Ms. Wilson:	I heard many of you notice the corners, the pointy parts. We call these shapes "polygons" because they all are made with corners and straight sides—not like your other shapes. These [points to the curved shapes] are different from polygons, they don't have corners and they don't have straight sides. How many sides do these have?
D:	You can't roll that one [points to the irregular closed curve].
Ms. Wilson:	That's true, but can you run your finger along the outside of the shape—do you come to a corner? Camille, try that—how many corners does the circle have?
C:	It goes around and around.
Ms. Wilson:	Right, so we say it only has one side. You can count the sides on the other shapes. What about the corners on the shapes in your two piles? Do all of your pointy shapes have corners? [The students move the shapes about and agree that all the shapes on their second mat have corners.]
Ms. Wilson:	Great! Now, I'll push them all together and you start again and this time have a different way to sort—to put them into piles with a *different* reason. [Teacher moves the shapes together.] You're working well together and I am very interested to see what you'll come up with next. [Teacher moves on to another group.]
L:	I like the long ones. [Takes rectangle and "long" right triangle and puts them in one pile.]

[The discussion continues.]

■ DISCUSSION OF THE MATHEMATICS TEACHING EXAMPLE

Mathematics Goals

The main mathematical goal in the lesson is to have students increase their awareness of attributes of shapes; for example, existence of corners and straight or curved sides. The sorting activity helps students begin to notice properties, such as, "This has square corners," and informally define classes of shapes, as "These all have four sides." Formal terms such as *right angle* and *quadrilateral* cannot be learned until awareness of such properties has been developed.

Mathematical communication skills are fostered as students learn more about the meaning of sorting objects into two distinct groups and that a variety of sorting rules may be used for a set of objects. Students are learning to talk about mathematics by using conversational language to scaffold into formal mathematical language. They practice verbally justifying their decisions as to why certain shapes are grouped together.

Language Goals

Because the lesson is centered on active involvement, the teacher has many opportunities to model the expected structure, syntax, and vocabulary of conversational English and to use questions and sentence responses both during small-group and whole-class discussions. Clear language goals in this lesson are to have students speak and listen for the purpose of communicating. The activity provides a purposeful context for development of targeted conversational language. For example, students may make statements such as, "I want to be first," "Put it in the other pile," "Where is my paper?," and "Please give me some shapes."

Initial concept development and introduction of formal mathematical terms occur while using conversational language. Ms. Wilson models standard usage and formal terms, but she allows the students' conversation to go on without correcting students' choice of terms or lack of complete sentences; for example, students say, "Pointy;" "And round ones there." The teacher builds on students' knowledge of everyday English terms, such as *piles,* to explain the assignment, and the students use language that they know as they complete the assignment.

Math and language goals are intertwined. Ms. Wilson is conscious of the language that she uses and anticipates possible breaks in understanding. She demonstrates purposeful use of familiar words such as *treasures* to initially introduce the word *sorting,* and then she later uses the word *shapes* with *sorting.* She alternates between using the term *sorting,* and the class's definition, *putting into piles with a reason,* as she focuses attention on how the shapes are alike and different.

Students of Varying Language Proficiency Levels Working Together

In this lesson, English learners work with English-only students. The English learners vary from beginning to advanced English-language proficiency levels, and all participate. The gamelike context sets students at ease and draws them in. The task is challenging and offers many possible ways of sorting. This gives the students many things to talk about in their small groups. Because the task involves objects that can be picked up and moved, some communication between students also occurs through gesturing. Making reference to a specific shape provides a context for understanding when a classmate says "sharp" or "pointy."

Interestingly, Camille appears to be searching for a general term to apply to all of the polygons when she refers to boxes. Her classmates do not pick up on this word, most likely because they are focusing on their own mathematical needs, and not because of any language barrier. Such a dialogue could easily occur in a group of fluent first or second graders.

Talking and Doing Help With Thinking

By hearing the other students refer to the "pointy" shapes, Ernesto becomes more aware of geometric attributes, particularly the existence of corners. Language, including both formal and informal terms, helps learners to think in new ways and to internalize their thought processes. Discussing, and even arguing, helps students clarify their thinking, solidify their understanding, and at the same time provides language development opportunities. For example, at the beginning of the lesson, Ms. Wilson says to the students, "Everyone, tell your neighbor what we called 'putting into piles for a reason.' What does it mean?"

Throughout the lesson, there are many specific ideas to see and discuss, because the lesson is centered around active involvement and concrete materials. For example, the students become more aware of curved and straight sides and of vertices (corners). They also go further to investigate similarities and differences between the octagon and a circle.

Developing Awareness of Attributes of Geometric Shapes

Through a group activity involving considerable use of conversational language, as well as manipulation of cardboard shapes, the four students with varying levels of English proficiency make considerable progress in expanding their awareness of attributes. Some of the students may not have ever focused on corners or curved sides before this activity. (Interestingly, it is quite possible that the students are still not aware of the existence of angles in the polygons, as students' geometric perception develops with increased experience.) But, the students all go beyond vague nonmathematical statements such as, "It looks like a triangle," to describing attributes as a means of justifying their groupings. For example, they are likely to be able to say, with support, "These are all polygons because they are made with straight sides that touch." Such statements eventually lead to the ability to make informal proofs.

Young children need to touch, move, and talk about geometric shapes in order to become aware of attributes. Worksheets with pictures of shapes do not lead to the same level of learning.

■ TEACHING TIPS

- Create a classroom climate where students' collaboration and conversation about mathematical ideas are valued and where students take turns speaking in a group and sharing their thinking.
- Teach students to listen to one another's ideas and to build on each other's statements. Post and model use of sentence starters such as, "I agree with Ali that there are . . .," "I'd like to build on Jenna's idea . . .," and "I don't understand what Kira meant when she said . . ."
- Teach students how to involve classmates with limited English proficiency in group work by using gestures, pictures, questions, and short clear statements.
- Present small groups of students with pure and applied mathematics problems that provoke students' interest and naturally lead to discussion and to communication through the use of visual representations such as diagrams or manipulatives.
- Ask students whether they agree or disagree with a statement; ask them to compare and contrast two related ideas.

Figure 1.3   Sample sentence starters can be provided to expand English learners' participation in class discussions.

- "I notice that . . ."
- "I agree with   (name)   that there are . . ."
- "I'd like to build on   (name)'s   idea . . ."
- "I don't understand what   (name)   meant when she said . . ."

- Increase students' opportunities to speak during class by interspersing lessons with brief Think-Pair-Share sessions in which both partners express their ideas to the best of their abilities. For example, "Tell your neighbor how you found your estimate for this problem."
- Give groups of students specific ideas and questions to discuss with one another, and also give suggested formats for reporting back. Alternate between asking for a group report and individual responses.

Figure 1.4 Tables and charts can teach organizational skills and also serve as a public record of words and ideas for English learners to talk about.

	Comparing Two Kids		
	Zach	*Rya*	
	brown hair	brown hair	*alike*
different	straight hair	curly hair	
different	glasses	no glasses	
	pants	pants	*alike*
different	T-shirt	buttoned shirt	
different	red sweater	blue sweater	

- Ask questions that address a variety of levels of thinking, including factual, application, analysis, synthesis, interpretive, and predictive questions so that students of varying language fluency levels have opportunities to both speak and listen.
- Develop the habit of adding at least seven seconds of wait time after asking a question.
- Use routines and procedures for asking various students for their response so that all children get a chance to speak, while no one is forced to do so.
- Allow mixed use of language (primary language along with English) during students' mathematics discussions.

DISCUSSION OF CONVERSATIONAL LANGUAGE

Students' conversational language skills can be enhanced during mathematics instructional time. At the same time, the use of informal language can support mathematical learning. Mathematics lessons should be designed to purposefully add to students' English conversational language skills. This may include purposeful instructions to focus on language related to specific contexts such as using polite sentences to ask for things or instructions to use particular sentence frames during a lesson.

Promoting informal engagement in mathematical conversation is particularly useful in mathematics problem-solving lessons because it creates "social scaffolding" for English learners. Students can begin to be involved in higher-level mathematical work when a classroom culture and peers offer support from initial task comprehension to the exploration and investigation of different possible strategies and solutions. When small groups of children are left alone with a comprehensible, engaging task, the discussion goes in many directions, and the language used reflects whatever background knowledge the students have at that moment. Especially for English learners, the appropriate formal mathematical vocabulary must be layered on top of experiences, not presented abstractly.

Allowing students to use their primary language can help students at beginning levels of fluency sort out their ideas and remain engaged in learning the targeted concepts and skills. Mixed language use, when communicating complex new ideas, allows English learners to get their message across (Moschkovich, in press).

Why is conversational language important in learning mathematics?

Children in school settings almost always acquire conversational language skills earlier than academic language. This language can be used to describe ideas and to ask questions during mathematics lessons. For example, when discussing a division word problem, a student might say, "They share; everyone get the same." Such language can help connect known ideas from everyday life, such as sharing items, to new math concepts such as division. Conversational language can also serve as an important tool in presenting mathematical arguments and making generalizations.

Discussing mathematical ideas supports the development of mathematical understanding. All students are encouraged to fully participate in lessons when a teacher establishes classroom norms and expectations for class discussions, helps everyone focus on the mathematical content of what is being discussed, supports students' attempts to speak up through rephrasing and clarifying, and builds on students' statements.

Conversational language also helps students interact with one another in the classroom, thus helping to engage English learners in learning activities. Additionally, English words and phrases that are useful both in and out of the classroom can be reinforced during mathematics lessons. Examples include *work together, fair, share, put away, pass out,* and *take turns.*

Why is a problem-solving approach to mathematics helpful to English learners' language development?

Problem solving involves more than one- or two-step word problems, or computation in context. It has been defined as figuring out what to do when you don't know what to do. Problem solving can provide a reason for students to strive to communicate in a second language (Dominguez, 2005). In spite of language challenges, grappling with nonroutine problems can be profitable both for language and for mathematics learning. Students engage in considerable linguistic activity and compare and contrast mathematical ideas as they work together to solve a problem. In addition, there are opportunities to deepen understanding as students are asked to defend their reasoning (for example, "The reason I know my answer is correct is because . . ."); to extend the problem to find patterns, mathematical rules, or generalizations; and to discuss connections to other problems.

What are characteristics of effective prompts for stimulating conversational language?

Effective prompts are understandable, motivating, challenging yet not out of reach, and have multiple ways of being represented and thought about. Easy tasks are often dismissed without much discussion, whereas prompts where the solution is not readily apparent are much more likely to lead to healthy arguments and counterarguments and verbal clarification of ideas. When a task lends itself to multiple representations such as tables, graphs, diagrams, and equations, students encounter a variety of ways of making sense and deepening their understanding.

Tasks may have some aspects that need to be clarified at the outset. Students may need some explicit help to enhance the motivational aspects that will intrigue and engage them, just as they may need some scaffolding to help them see connections to related situations and mathematical ideas.

Note that textbooks have interesting problems that can spark conversation in sections such as Problem of the Day, Thinker's Corner, Practice Problems, and Extensions.

How can you ensure that all children will have a chance to speak and to ask questions?

This is a critical responsibility of the teacher and hinges on decisions regarding the establishment of classroom norms, use of questioning techniques, and training of students in specific classroom roles and working cooperatively with classmates. Classroom norms, or rules of conduct, should be established at the beginning of the year through classroom discussion, rehearsal, and practice and referred to regularly throughout the year.

Many teachers have found that when they retrain themselves to avoid repeatedly calling on the most eager students and to avoid giving praise after each student utterance, they are able to encourage the quieter students to join in and the most eager students to be respectful of their peers' ideas as well as their peers' needs to participate.

Some teachers use simple systems such as randomly pulling name-sticks from a container in order to invite students to speak up and to protect think-time (wait-time) for all students. More students have an opportunity to voice their thoughts when Think-Pair-Shares are used frequently to provide think-time for a moment, nonthreatening talk-time with one partner, and then sharing out with a larger group (Lyman, 2003). Also, small-group assignments to synthesize, or even to list the ideas of group members, provide opportunities for most or all students to speak up in a relatively nonthreatening setting.

Cooperative groups are used by many teachers as venues for increasing opportunities to speak and for taking turns with responsibilities and roles. They can give students a relatively low-risk chance to take turns leading a group, writing down a group's ideas, reporting back to the class as a whole, and so on. Students who are beyond the very beginning levels of language acquisition can take on a group responsibility and speak to their group-mates and class with the support of a buddy or an adult helper. It is important to clearly state expectations as to group organization, individual and group responsibilities, and planned format for showing results.

■ CONVERSATIONAL LANGUAGE RESEARCH

In an overview of research, Genesee, Lindholm-Leary, Saunders, and Christian (2005) found several strong benefits from the promotion of oral language skills in a second language. Not surprisingly, increased oral language skills are associated with increases in use of the second language and further increases in proficiency. Oral proficiency is related to the ability to use more complex language learning strategies, including interacting with others and monitoring speech, which can be of particular importance in the mathematics classroom. Also, higher-level question forms are used and the ability to define words increases when oral language skills are promoted.

According to Cummins (2000), students acquire language in phases. The first and easier phase is Basic Interpersonal Communications Skills (BICS). In this phase, students develop social language skills. They may carry on a conversation with a friend, ask for directions, or play a game. BICS is typically developed within familiar, interactive, and uncomplicated contexts.

The second, and more difficult phase, is Cognitive Academic Language Skills (CALPS). CALPS includes much more than the learning of formal mathematics terms. It involves types of thinking and communicating that are uniquely found inside the school. In this phase, students use the language of the classroom. For example, they describe, compare, justify, or synthesize content information and use academic vocabulary.

Traditionally, mathematical academic language skills have been taught during instruction on cognitively demanding new concepts and skills, through context-reduced communicative activities (Chamot & O'Malley, 1994). In addition, Gersten and Baker (2001) point to research showing the very limited amount of class time that is spent speaking or writing in English, even in English Language Development classrooms. Teachers of English learners are now changing their mathematics instruction to increase overall use of both conversational and academic language and to make instruction more accessible through the use of a variety of strategies, as described in this book and others (Herrell & Jordan, 2004). One strategy is for the teacher to monitor and adjust his own speech so that the pace and sentence structure make students' comprehension more likely (Echevarria, Vogt, & Short, 2004).

Krashen and Terrell (1983; Krashen, 2002) contend that having opportunities for purposeful use of language supports its development and expansion in a natural way. Models have been developed in response to the argument that English learners need frequent opportunities to express complex ideas in English. These include the Instructional Conversation Model, Complex Instruction, and Brenner's Communication Framework. The Instructional Conversation Model not only promotes considerable use of oral language through teacher questions and statements, but its primary purpose is to teach complex concepts and to develop learning habits such as analysis, reflection, and critical thinking (Goldenberg, 1991; Khisty & Viego, 2005). The Complex Instruction model based on the work of Edward de Avila and Sharon Duncan has students working in groups as they complete tasks. This peer-to-peer teaching and learning model was further developed by Elizabeth Cohen (1994). Brenner's (1994) Communication Framework encourages students to discuss, argue, and communicate about mathematics.

Cooperative learning groups have been used extensively in language arts instruction (Kagan, Kagan, & Kagan, 2000; Nelson, 1996) and in science (Cohen, 1994) but have not been extensively researched with English learners and mathematics (Siegler, 2003). Cohen (1994), Cohen and Lotan (1997), Johnson and Johnson (1990), Marzano, Norford, Paynter, Pickering, and Gaddy (2001), and Siegler (2003) all point out the importance of carefully structuring and nurturing effective work in cooperative groups. Boaler (2006) discusses the importance of the teacher's expectations, encouragement, and explicit fostering of critical learning practices during group work sessions. Boaler also brings forth the crucial need to build relational equity among students by addressing issues of status through mathematics lessons where different insights, methods, and perspectives are valued.

Goal 2 of the ESL Standards for PreK–12 Students calls for students to use English to achieve academically in all content areas (Teachers of English to Speakers of Other Languages [TESOL], 1997). Goal 3 requires teachers to provide students with opportunities to use English in socially and culturally appropriate ways. Cooperative groups provide one setting where students can address these goals as they listen to, speak about, demonstrate, and act out their ideas. Cooperative groups are a less threatening setting to practice speaking, to ask questions, as well as to hear peers' models of spoken English. Cooperative learning groups increase students' opportunities to be actively involved and to compare mathematical strategies (Cohen, 1994). Both conversational and academic language usage increases. Also, motivation is likely to increase when both group responsibility (positive interdependence) and individual accountability are expected (Nelson, 1996). It is important to group students heterogeneously so that each group represents various levels of English fluency (Chamot & O'Malley, 1994).

Research indicates that when the community and educational institution value primary/native language and give specific supports to aid English acquisition, students' academic success is greater (Tse, 2001). Especially when problem solving is done as a small-group project, and when the topics are culturally relevant, English learners do better in school, both in their native language and target language.

■ PRACTICE AND DISCUSSION QUESTIONS

1. How can you be sure that all discourse in your mathematics class meets the needs of all of your EL students? Give some examples.

2. What are your thoughts about the goals and suggestions in this chapter? What goals and suggestions are most important for your classroom? Describe how you plan to implement specific ideas in your classroom.

3. What behaviors are important for a class to develop in order to maximize language development opportunities during mathematics lessons? Give examples of specific things that you would promote in your classroom.

4. Identify one key concept for a particular grade. How might you use a problem-solving approach and small-group work to promote both the learning of the concept and English language acquisition? Give specific examples and plans.

2

Developing Academic Language

Develop Mathematics Concepts and Vocabulary for English Learners

RATIONALE FROM RESEARCH ■

People use different types of language in the different contexts of their lives. Mathematics, as an academic discipline, is made up of concepts that are most effectively discussed with proficiency in academic language.

Academic language in mathematics instruction includes the specialized words and phrases related to content, procedures, the activity of learning, and expression of complex thinking processes. Echevarria, Vogt, and Short (2004) explain Cummins's term, Cognitive Academic Language Proficiency (CALP), as "the abstract language abilities required for academic work. A more complex, conceptual, linguistic ability that includes analysis, synthesis and evaluation" (p. 221). Barnett-Clarke and Ramirez (2004) point out, "Not only do students need explicit instruction to read and write mathematical symbols and words, they also need to learn how to express mathematical ideas orally and with written symbols" (p. 57). Rubenstein and Thompson (2001) add that being able to read symbols is linked to understanding.

Teachers use strategies to develop both mathematical academic language and mathematical ideas. Learning new academic terms is a complex endeavor. Students benefit from multiple exposures to new terms in the course of meaningful activities (Bielenberg & Wong Fillmore, 2005) and from multiple support systems, including activities with visual and tactile scaffolding, as is illustrated in the following teaching example.

In the following teaching example, a set of typical textbook word problems for the second grade prompts the teacher to develop a special lesson.

■ MATHEMATICS TEACHING EXAMPLE

Word Problems

Number Riddles

Solve each riddle.

1. Kai has 6 dollars. Her brother has 10 dollars. How many more dollars does the brother have?

2. Kai has 40 baseball cards. Her brother has 15 fewer cards. How many baseball cards does her brother have?

3. Kai is 10 years old. Her brother is 3 years younger. How old is the brother?

4. Kai bought a special book for 5 dollars. Did this increase or decrease her savings? *Fill in the blanks:*

This _____ creased her money by _____ dollars. She had _____ dollars left.
   (in- / de-)   (more / fewer)

Jake Blue teaches a second-grade class that includes several English learners of varying fluency levels. He is modifying the textbook assignment in the teaching example for his class. He prepares posters with the following headings to write notes with the class: *More, Less, Fewer, Increase, Decrease.* As he prepares the lesson, he decides that his main goals for the day will be to work on "more" and "less/fewer" relationships, saving attention for "increase" and "decrease" for a future lesson.

As the children sit down on the rug at the front of the room, Mr. Blue starts telling a story to engage the students. "When I was in second grade, I saved up money and one day I had five dollars. Help me count these dollars: one, two, three, four, five. My older brother was always teasing me, and he told me that he had two more dollars than I did. We can write 'I had five dollars. My brother had two more dollars than me.' I will draw a diagram of my five-dollar bills all lined up.

"Now I am wondering, how many dollars did my brother have? How many dollars should I draw for my brother? Talk to your neighbor for a minute. . . . I'll take a quiet hand from someone who can explain." Many students declare that the brother had seven dollars, some showing "five and two more" on their fingers or with linking cubes. Mr. Blue draws his brother's seven dollars next to his five dollars and labels the diagram, with a line showing that they both have at least five dollars.

"We can use our linking cubes and also diagrams like this [Figure 2.1] to *compare* two numbers to see how they are different, to find the *difference*. What was the difference between my money and my brother's money? . . . Yes, the difference was the 'two more dollars' that he had. Our amounts of money were different by two dollars." Mr. Blue writes the expression "5 + 2" on the "More" poster and explains, "Today we'll be working on how we use the words *more* and *less* in math problems."

"What if I had saved a different number of dollars? Let's do some examples. I'll say a number for my dollars. AJ, you go first and use blue linking cubes to show my dollars. Then, everyone think how many yellow cubes should Pablo show for my brother's dollars? Remember, my brother has two more than my number, like these two red cubes more. I'll start with five. What are you thinking for two more than five?" Mr. Blue does several turns and asks the whole class to respond together. Each time, the two students show their cube towers next to one another. Gradually, Mr. Blue draws attention to the "more cubes" by asking the students to use two red cubes to show "the brother's extras." He comments, "My blue cube tower needs two more cubes to match my brother's tower. The difference is two cubes."

Figure 2.1   Mr. Blue's diagram comparing the number of dollar bills.

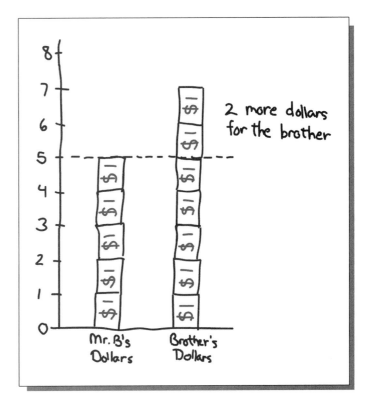

Next, Mr. Blue asks students to model a problem with the starting amount of six dollars and the difference "four more." He asks, "What should we record if I have six dollars and my brother has four more dollars than me?" (6 + 4). Mr. Blue talks aloud as he constructs a bar diagram, emphasizing that in math problems like this, "We can think about the amount that is the same, or that 'matches,' and then we can tell 'the more part' and add to find the total of the larger amount."

"Now let's all practice saying the whole equation. For example, I could say, 'Four more than six equals ten.' Let's go back to our 'two more than' rule. [He holds up a printed card.] I'll say a number and then I'll call on someone who will say the whole equation. For example, if I say 'Six,' then you would say, 'Two more than six equals eight.'" During oral practice, Mr. Blue records a number sentence for what each student says. Then, he writes "6 + 2 = 8" and tells the students that one way to read this number

Figure 2.2   A bar diagram for a comparison problem when the difference is given.

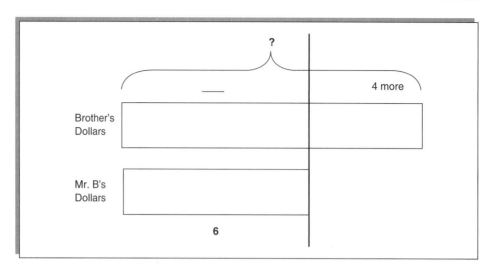

sentence is to say, "Two more than six equals eight." He asks, "Who noticed that the order of the numbers in the equation and of the sentence on the poster are not the same?" He works through a few examples with the class, and returns to having students show linking cube representations to point out the amount that matches and using the words *difference, how they are different,* and *how much more.*

To shift attention to problems where the difference needs to be found, Mr. Blue says, "Now I'm going to use the word *more* again, but this time we will need to find out something else, so listen carefully. Once I had five dollars and my brother had seven dollars. How many more dollars did my brother have?" Mr. Blue draws two bars on the poster as a visual tool for giving meaning to the problem question.

"What do we need to figure out?" Mr. Blue encourages class discussion and focuses students' attention on comments such as "How they are different," "How much more money," and "How much extra money." The

Figure 2.3   A diagram is used to communicate the problem situation and to give meaning to several related phrases.

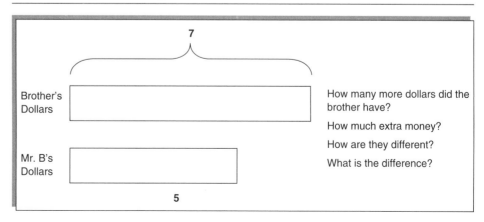

students practice labeling the diagram and pointing out the part of the diagram that refers to the difference. Mr. Blue says, "This part is the answer to the question, 'How many more dollars?' "

"Talk to your neighbor about how you figured out the answer." Students share strategies that include counting up to see how many more dollars Mr. Blue needed to match his brother, thinking about what number goes with five to equal seven, and modeling with cubes. Mr. Blue reminds the students that their ways can be written both with the number sentences $5 + 2 = 7$ and $7 - 5 = 2$, which he records on the poster. But, he realizes that future lessons will need to build meaning for the idea of using subtraction to represent "how many more" and "the difference between" when two amounts are given.

"Now, see what is different about this problem: Once I had five dollars and my brother had seven dollars. How many fewer dollars did I have? How is this problem different?" The class refers to the bar diagram and points to who has fewer dollars, who has more. Mr. Blue says, "Tell your partner two things that you know about the problem that goes with this diagram. Put up a finger when you hear your partner say 'different,' 'difference,' 'less,' 'fewer,' or 'more.'" Afterward, Mr. Blue told the class, "I heard several of you notice that I would need to get two more dollars to equal my brother's seven dollars and that the difference is two dollars, just like in our other problem. Alan, please use our diagram to talk about that idea. . . . I heard some students say, 'Mr. Blue has two fewer dollars.' Kamilah, please use our diagram to show us why that idea makes sense."

"We should talk more about our other words for today, *less* and *fewer*. *Fewer* and *less* both tell us that there isn't as much. It's the opposite of having more. Sometimes problems say 'two less than' or 'two fewer' instead of telling about 'more.' For example, our problem could say that my brother had seven dollars and I had two fewer dollars. Then the question is how much money did I have; or, how much is two fewer dollars than seven dollars? Look, if I write $7 - 2$, we can read this is as 'two fewer than seven' or 'two less than seven.' We'll be learning more about that. Who can remind us how our bar diagram tells how much is two *less* than seven?

"Now let's practice saying complete sentences and showing equations. For example, if I say, 'Maria has four dollars and José has six dollars,' you would say, 'José has two more dollars than Maria. Maria has two fewer dollars than José. The difference is two dollars.'" Mr. Blue writes the frame of these sentences and equations on the board:

_____ has __ dollars and _____ has __ dollars. _____ has ___ *more* dollars than _____. _____ has ___ *fewer* dollars than _____.

The difference is __ dollars.

__ + __ = __ and __ − __ = __.

Mr. Blue then gives students a few more examples orally, has them discuss each one with a partner, asks a few students to share their thinking, and records the equations.

During the next lesson, Mr. Blue uses the same sentence frames and introduces a simple game to practice working with *more* and *less* comparison relationships. Students work with a partner and use two number cubes and their own small name cards. The first partner rolls the first number cube and places it on the first number spot on the sentence frame, and the second partner does the same for the second number of dollars. The students work together to figure out the answers and write the complete sentences and equations on their own papers. They become skilled at the oral part of the activity, but show some confusion about the number sentences.

During the game, Mr. Blue goes from group to group. At one group he says, "I just heard you say 'three more.' Did you figure that out by adding or subtracting?" The student responds, "I added on." Mr. Blue asks, "So what's the equation then?" When he gets a response of "two and three more equals five," he says, "Great! Write it down. Keep going." He moves to another group and says, "I just heard you say, 'Maria has more dollars.' How many more?" Mr. Blue continues with this type of interaction as the game progresses.

Next, Mr. Blue draws the students' attention to the four "number riddles." He has a whole-class brainstorming session on ways to show how to solve the first problem as a way of reviewing the language, models, diagrams, and number sentences used the previous day. Then, he hands out the problems to each student and asks them to work in their small groups as they solve the problems and to show on their papers different ways of thinking about each problem.

■ DISCUSSION OF THE MATHEMATICS TEACHING EXAMPLE

Mathematics Goals

The goals of this lesson are to help students understand and interpret word problems involving additive comparisons of two distinct quantities and to understand related mathematical academic language terms such as *more, less,* and *fewer*. A secondary goal is to use multiple representations to demonstrate how additive or subtractive comparison relationships can be represented using language (for example, word problems), diagrams, and symbols (for example, equations). Also, during the lesson, connections between addition and subtraction are reinforced in several ways and a foundation is built for future work with word problems involving fractions and decimals. The students begin to see mathematical similarities between various word problems.

Mr. Blue introduces the class to a new meaning for the symbolic expression, "6 + 2," when he writes it to represent two more dollars than the six that he started with. He also teaches students how to read such symbolic expressions as saying "two more than six," noting that the digit 2 is after the 6, but it comes second in the symbolic expression. He apparently wants to prepare students for future algebraic expressions where $x + 2$ is interpreted as "two more than x." Of course, it may also be interpreted as "x and two more."

By first introducing the lesson with a situation involving "two more dollars than five," Mr. Blue is able to use it as a foundation for his representations for comparing two distinct amounts. The "two more dollars" represent the difference between his brother's amount of money and his amount of money.

Language Goals

A concurrent goal of this lesson is to develop students' ability to read and understand academic language in mathematics, particularly in relation to the specific terms *more, less, fewer, compare,* and *difference.* The mathematical meaning of the word difference is very carefully built and linked to the word *different.* Another goal is for students to develop their ability to use academic language in communicating with the teacher and other students and in solving and discussing simple mathematical problems.

Notice that the teacher models and writes frames of the sentences and equations as additional scaffolding for the desired use of the academic language. Also, several times, forms of response were simple enough for students at Proficiency Level 1 and Level 2 to participate, such as when showing a number of linking cubes or saying a particular sum.

Support Through Primary Language and Cognates

Whenever new concepts and language are introduced in the mathematics classroom, English learners need multiple support systems. In this lesson, new vocabulary is appropriately introduced through an activity with visual and tactile scaffolding. Students have a number of opportunities to communicate and verify their understanding. It is not clear whether all students, and particularly the beginning English speakers, understand the lesson since there is no mention of informal assessment nor observed use of primary language support. It is hoped that paraprofessionals, parent volunteers, older student-tutors, or classmates provide primary language support to the English learners during the initial phase of the lesson and during partner discussions. Use of primary language can increase opportunities to create links to prior knowledge in the student's primary language and increase the opportunity for every student to understand the foundational ideas of the lesson. Beginning English learners will also be able to verify their understanding of the new concepts if they know they can use their primary language to ask more complicated questions.

The teacher could point out that some words are very similar across languages, which are referred to as "cognates," or words that share a common root, for example, *diferencia* and *difference;* or *para comparar* and *to compare.*

The focus during mathematics instruction involving word problems is to read for meaning and to become aware of similarities between problems. Discussing a word problem in multiple languages can enhance the depth of understanding and make it possible for English learners to think about mathematical relationships in the primary language.

Developing Specific Math Vocabulary

In the teaching example, the students first experience the idea of "more" through discussion and hands-on modeling. The teacher posts a few targeted vocabulary words as headings on large class posters and has the class help develop explanations and illustrations. Even though the comparative words *more, less,* and *fewer* may be familiar in everyday contexts such as "I have more cookies," in this lesson they are indicating specific mathematical quantities such as "three less than. . . ." It may be helpful to point out to students the similarities and differences between "Who has fewer dollars?" and "How many fewer dollars does Maria have (than José)?"

The teacher made sure that new academic language was layered on top of the activity and discussion and that specific definitions and illustrations were jointly developed, discussed, posted, and referred to during the lesson. The teacher avoided the temptation to treat *more* and *fewer* as "key words" that magically say to add or subtract. Students might intuitively think that "more" indicates addition, but Mr. Blue carefully prepares them to see that in cases such as in Problem 1, "more" is part of a comparative phrase, "how many more." The phrase indicates that the difference between two amounts is to be found. This difference could be represented in a subtraction equation or as a missing addend problem. The consistent message to students is that they must read for meaning in a mathematics classroom, while developing facility with specific academic vocabulary.

Opportunities to Use Academic Language

The questions, verbal and physical models, diagrams, "talk to your neighbor" directions, and partner games all lead to an increased likelihood that students would have frequent meaningful encounters with the mathematics vocabulary. The positive environment and friendly, relaxed atmosphere also lead to the students' earnest efforts to learn the new concepts and words. When necessary, Mr. Blue scaffolds the students' sharing by repeating parts or all of the sentence frame used earlier in the lesson ("_____ has ___ more dollars than _____"). He asks the students to practice expressing their ideas using this frame.

When the students work in their small groups on the number riddles, Mr. Blue may systematically provide quick interactions and questions for students who need additional support as they attempt to use new mathematical academic language. He may plan when he will focus on specific students and when to model specific phrases when he interacts with these students.

Teaching Decisions

It is worth noting that the teacher chose to develop a lesson around four challenging word problems for his class that includes several English learners. He did not skip the important yet difficult topic of comparison problems. He uses word problems in order to develop this new mathematics concept and related academic language. By incorporating a variety of strategies and keeping the context interesting, yet simple, and the numbers small, the teacher is able to focus the students' attention on the vocabulary and the concepts.

Mr. Blue effectively balances between using "teachable moments" and waiting for a future opportunity to further discuss more abstract ideas. He keeps a tight time schedule, but manages to include several minutes of modeling, oral practice, and rehearsal at the beginning of the lesson. He checks all students' understanding on a regular basis. He has chosen to do a whole-class lesson, with modeling of several different representations during the main lesson, but without expecting students to immediately use the representations independently. He has decided to save the increase/decrease concept and vocabulary for another day. By constantly assessing the readiness of his students to take in more information, and through his informal observations and interactions with students during the lesson, Mr. Blue appropriately maintains the focus of the lesson and accomplishes reasonable goals and objectives with his students.

TEACHING TIPS ■

- Monitor adult use of language to ensure that it is positive and optimistic, in order to promote a safe environment where students feel comfortable taking risks to use mathematical language they are just learning, and where it is accepted that mistakes will occur while appropriate language use is being developed.
- Model proper mathematical use of language (for example, say "trapezoid" rather than "the red block") and incorporate rephrasing whenever speaking with students.
- Use choral response for single number or word answers. For example, say, "The shape on the wall that has only two parallel sides is a _____, everyone tell me."
- After a new concept has been developed, explicitly connect it to academic vocabulary.
- Explicitly encourage students to use new academic language by announcing, "Today, I'm listening for these words . . . ," then keep track of usage and record and share sample student sentences.

Figure 2.4   A word wall entry may be created as a part of a whole-class discussion once students are grasping the underlying concept.

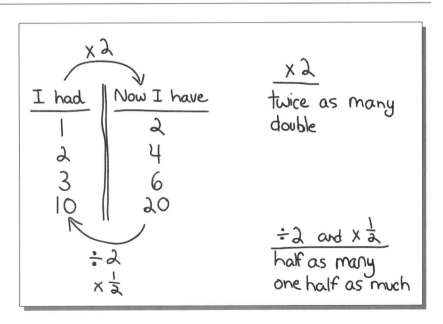

Figure 2.5   Students may be asked to fill out a word card as either a learning-support task or as a formative assessment task. The teacher varies the labels for the categories in order to maximize thinking about the particular word.

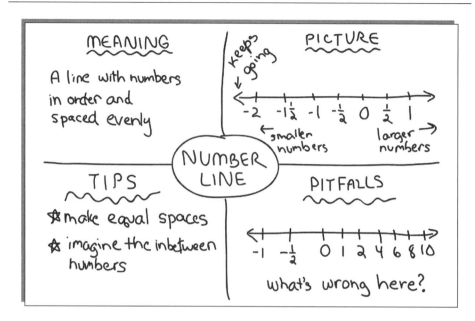

- Engage students in movement and use gestures that demonstrate actions associated with important verbs such as *combine,* when teaching concepts that underlie new vocabulary.
- Begin teaching a new concept through experiences that draw out and expand students' understanding, make use of informal language, and make explicit connections between student language and academic language; for example, help students' word *times-ing* become *multiplying.*
- Use visual aids such as a number line or a hundreds chart while teaching and practicing vocabulary and associated concepts such as less than, equivalent, and times as much.
- Introduce each word wall entry through a specific, interactive instructional process and refer frequently to individual word wall cards and posters. For example, work together with students to develop an illustrated poster that represents a new concept.
- Ask questions that are in a familiar repetitive frame, and model frames for appropriate responses while maintaining a focus on meaning and not repetition for its own sake.
- Ask groups of students to make statements that incorporate a desired phrase such as "twice as much as" as they analyze everyday items, such as the nutritional information written on two different cereal boxes.
- Create learning environments, and give enticing partner or small-group problem-solving assignments that compel students of various language abilities and varying levels of mathematical understanding to engage in meaningful use of mathematical language.
- Engage students in activities where they are asked to explain an idea or procedure to a younger student, or to give directions on how

to draw or locate an object, in order to promote use of mathematical language.

- Present students with problems that are incorrectly solved, tell them that the solution is incorrect, and ask them to discuss and explain the mistake and misunderstanding, and describe a correct solution method.

DISCUSSION OF ACADEMIC LANGUAGE DEVELOPMENT

Mathematics vocabulary words and phrases generally are *abstract* terms that relate to critically important concepts, often concepts that are not yet understood. Truly understanding and using such vocabulary may be one indication of success in learning a major new idea. In contrast, being able to repeat a definition of a mathematics term does not necessarily indicate understanding of the concept. Moschkovich (2002) points out that true proficiency with academic language involves much more than learning vocabulary and phrases. Students should also learn communication skills such as explaining and justifying mathematical ideas. A wide variety of mathematics assessment practices should be used to establish what students actually know.

Some mathematics vocabulary, such as *odd, area*, and *operations*, have specialized meanings that must be pointed out as different from everyday usage and that must be carefully taught like any other academic vocabulary associated with a new abstract idea. Other mathematics vocabulary may represent a word, with its concept, that is already understood in students' primary language. In such cases, links need to be made through discussion and illustration to associate the new English word with the known concept. For example, the Spanish word *cuadrilátero* supports the development of meaning for the English word *quadrilateral* because *cuatro lados* literally means "four sides."

Why is it usually not productive to go over new key vocabulary at the beginning of a math lesson?

In language arts, we want children to be able to read new material without being distracted by unfamiliar vocabulary. Therefore, presenting and discussing vocabulary words before the students read the new material helps them understand the material by "front-loading vocabulary." This strategy is often not as productive in mathematics. Mathematics vocabulary words often represent the main idea of an entire chapter or unit of study, while a new reading word is usually a supporting contextual element. For example, presenting a vocabulary word such as circumference to students as "the distance around a circle" will not be meaningful unless students have prerequisite understanding of distance as a one-dimensional measurement of length, and clear understanding of perimeter. An entire lesson may be centered on teaching the concept, and its word, *circumference*.

A new math *concept* that underlies a vocabulary word must be systematically built up through experiences, through activation of prior knowledge, and use of informal language. In addition, the formal vocabulary must be purposefully associated with the new concept and frequently practiced.

Consider the word *parallel*. What reaction and long-range success would you expect if you taught a fourth-grade lesson by focusing on a formal dictionary definition of parallel lines? How else might you start a lesson on parallel lines? For example, you might ask students to draw two lines that "stay the same distance apart" to represent train tracks or as a space for writing a heading on a poster. Students could physically check the measurements between the lines. You might say, "Talk with your partner about what you know about parallel lines, lines that stay the same distance apart. If you could draw very, very long lines, would they cross? Where?" As the concept of parallel becomes part of each student's experience, the formal vocabulary *parallel lines* can be introduced and associated with its physical meaning. As a product of such a class discussion, a wall poster might be made about parallel lines, using both academic and informal language as well as illustrations.

Why is it suggested that we not emphasize key words in math problems?

When students are encouraged to focus on key phrases such as "in all," "how many," and "less," they often fail to focus carefully on the meaning of a story problem, on the mathematical structure implied and what operation actually makes sense. Relying on key words leads to mistakes in choice of operation when such common phrases are used for a different purpose, such as, "In all of the boxes there were some . . ." or ". . . Then, Jim had five fewer stickers, so he only had eleven left. How many did he start with?" A key word focus also leads to a general lack of individual skill at interpreting story problems, identifying the underlying mathematical relationships, and making plans for a solution.

In reality, there are not very many types of situations that are commonly associated with each operation, so it makes sense to help students focus on understanding such key relationships as part-part-total addition and subtraction situations, and sharing, or partitive, division situations, rather than focusing on key words. When the focus is on understanding the action involved and the mathematical relationships behind important phrases such as "three times as many," students are more likely to be able to generalize to other problems and to find a solution no matter which quantity is the missing quantity in a problem.

Why do we need to differentiate discussion goals for levels of English language development?

Students of varying proficiency levels can engage in the same mathematics investigations and lessons. However, ability to *speak* about the mathematics and to use the new target vocabulary will vary according to language level. A student at Proficiency Level 2 is likely to understand spoken language and to model "three more than six" with cubes or possibly to answer, "It's nine." Students at Level 3 or Level 4 are more able to initiate use of a newly posted target phrase such as "half of" with a statement such as, "Look, five is half of ten!" They are also more able to refer to posted discussion phrases such as, "I know this is correct, because . . ." to explain their reasoning in general terms.

A lesson plan should include carefully planned opportunities to learn about and to use new vocabulary in a meaningful context. Questions and instructions should vary between literal and complex forms. Students at beginning levels of language proficiency can be encouraged to respond orally to simply stated questions, while students at more advanced levels will benefit from clear, interesting questions that entice them to speak and to use new vocabulary. All students should be thinking about the same important, high-level mathematics.

ACADEMIC LANGUAGE RESEARCH   ■

It can take five to seven years for students to acquire academic English at a level that enables them to fully benefit from academic instruction in English (Cummins, 2000). Given the complex nature of mathematical academic language, and the ever-increasing content demands across the grades, it is not surprising that it takes considerable time, and purposeful teaching, for academic English to be fully acquired.

Academic language for mathematics involves much more than learning vocabulary. Solomon and Rhodes (1995) discuss various ways that researchers describe academic language. They point out that Cummins and many others emphasize that academic language is less context-embedded in nature than conversational language (BICS) and is associated with high cognitive demand. Others stress that academic language is a compilation of unique language functions and structures. Examples of language functions are comparing, classifying, predicting, justifying, persuading, and solving problems. Dale and Cuevas (1987) point out examples of special mathematical syntactic structures such as comparative structures (for example, greater than four) and logical connectors (for example, if . . . then . . .). Besides language functions, Spanos, Rhodes, Dale, and Crandall (1988) point out the importance of technical vocabulary terms, complex strings of words, ordinary vocabulary that has different meanings in math, and synonymous words and phrases (for example, *add, plus,* and *combine*), and various mathematical symbols and notations. The teachers in Solomon and Rhodes's study tended to focus on academic language "in terms of discrete aspects of language, such as vocabulary, lexis, and syntax," particularly in terms of the language students need to understand the lesson or unit being studied, as opposed to more theoretical components.

Barnett-Clarke and Ramirez (2004) bring up the importance of language when thinking about mathematics, using what Bickmore-Brand (1990) calls "internal chatter." Teachers can model this kind of reflective talk as they work through a problem that presents a challenge to their students. Internal chatter may occur in English, in the primary language, or in a combination of languages. The important point is that knowing academic terms and phrases facilitates thinking, learning, and problem solving.

■ PRACTICE AND DISCUSSION QUESTIONS

1. Think about the vocabulary term *greater than* and its symbol. How would you teach it to second graders?

2. Name a specific academic language term or terms and a targeted grade level. Describe what you would do to maximize students' acquisition and use of the term(s) during a lesson.

3. Why is it advisable to teach vocabulary through movement and action to English learners? What else should be done?

4. How can you ensure that English learners use academic language as they participate in oral discourse?

3
Scaffolding

Give Support for Both
Mathematics and Language Learning

RATIONALE FROM RESEARCH ■

In the early twentieth century, Vygotsky pointed out that

> in studies of children's mental development it is generally
> assumed that only those things that children can do on their own
> are indicative of mental abilities. . . . On the other hand, if we offer
> leading questions . . . what children can do with the assistance of
> others might be in some sense even more indicative of their mental
> development than what they can do alone. This difference . . . the
> zone of proximal development . . . is the distance between the
> actual developmental level as determined by independent problem
> solving and the level of potential development as determined
> through problem solving under adult guidance or in collaboration
> with more capable peers. (Vygotsky, 1978, pp. 85–86)

Vygotsky emphasizes the importance for a child's learning to be guided
thoughtfully by a knowledgeable adult or more capable peer. The learning and problem solving that can occur are at a level of difficulty beyond
what the learner can do independently (Vygotsky, 1978). This type of
guidance is often termed "scaffolding" (Wood, Bruner, & Ross, 1976).

Echevarria, Vogt, and Short (2004) point out three types of scaffolding that are particularly helpful to English learners: verbal scaffolding, which helps advance language skills; procedural scaffolding, which includes modeling and coaching; and instructional scaffolding, which includes graphic organizers to enhance comprehension. For the mathematics teacher, scaffolding involves preplanning ways to enhance a specific lesson so that students maximize their learning of mathematics concepts and skills, and of language, during the lesson time. Think of how ineffective it usually is for a teacher to simply verbally explain, demonstrate, and then assign practice work to a class on a new skill. What would a master teacher do? A teacher scaffolds a lesson to ensure that students learn at a deeper level by incorporating visual learning strategies, concrete materials, demonstrations, questioning, and other appropriate methods (Echevarria et al., 2004).

Scaffolding helps with both English development and mathematics learning. Scaffolding academic language contributes to English learners' language fluency. It creates a foundation for more effective verbal interactions. Scaffolding mathematics lessons involves students in meaningful, active learning experiences and creates contexts for significant use of language. Just as Krashen and Terrell (1983) emphasize the importance of using language in a natural and meaningful context, the National Council of Teachers of Mathematics (NCTM) and the National Research Council emphasize the need to learn mathematics in an environment where ideas make sense and where work is sufficiently challenging (NCTM, 2000; National Research Council, 2001).

Scaffolding academic language is necessary throughout all levels of acquiring fluency in the target language (Gibbons, 1993). This scaffolding spans content ability levels as well as grade levels. Scaffolding of mathematics learning can occur from preschool through college levels.

■ MATHEMATICS TEACHING EXAMPLE

Algebraic Reasoning

Table Arrangement Problem

Antonio and Maria have two different ways to arrange square tables. Only one person can sit on each side of one of the tables.

Antonio's Way: Keep the tables separate
Maria's Way: Push the tables together in a long, narrow row

Your group's job:

Investigate Antonio's table arrangement plan and then Maria's plan.

A. With your group, *make a two-column chart* for each plan.

Show the *number of tables* and the *number of seats for people* if Antonio and Maria use 1, 2, 3, 4, 5, or 10 tables.

B. Think about Antonio's plan if 40 people come.

How many tables would they need?

How can you easily figure out how many people will sit at any number of tables?

Tell how you know in a sentence. Also, write an equation (number sentence).

C. Think about Maria's plan if 40 people come. How many tables would they need?

Draw a diagram. Explain how you figured it out.

A fourth-grade teacher of a class with many English learners at various proficiency levels developed this lesson for his class and included it in his teaching portfolio. He submitted the following report on the lesson:

I didn't start by passing out the problem. Instead, I started with an engaging story, presented slowly and with plenty of gestures: "Remember when we had all the students and their adults here for the party in the fall? We let people sit where they wanted, anywhere in the room, and it worked fine. Well, there once was another class, and they were having a special kind of party called a banquet." I explained that a "banquet" is a kind of fancy party, and everyone had to sit down together. "So, the students in that class were thinking about how to arrange the tables for their banquet. Two students, Antonio and Maria, were having different ideas about how to arrange the tables. They knew the space for the banquet would be a long hallway. Antonio thought that the tables should be separate. Maria thought they should be pushed together. The problem is that they didn't really know how many people would come. They thought that maybe 40 people would come, but their teacher wanted to be able to figure out how many tables would be needed for each plan, for any number of people that said they would come. How could they figure this out?"

Next, I put one desk in the front of the classroom and put a tablecloth over it. "Let's have students come up and stand by this pretend table like it was at the banquet. Sara, Mai, Samuel, Rigo, you come and stand here. Everyone tell me, how many people can sit at one table." ("Four.")

I continued, "Now what if we get another table?" I put another tablecloth on another desk. "Tracy, Ricky, Lan, Eva, you come up and you'll be at the next table. This is Antonio's plan, right? Everyone, show me on your fingers how many can sit at two tables."

"Now, what if we follow Maria's plan? She wants to push the tables together. So let's do that." (I dragged the second table and the students helped.) "It looks like Ricky has to move away and so does Mai. What happened? How many can sit at two tables now, when they're pushed together? Everyone, show me on your fingers."

Figure 3.1   The teacher drew illustrations as the ideas were explained.

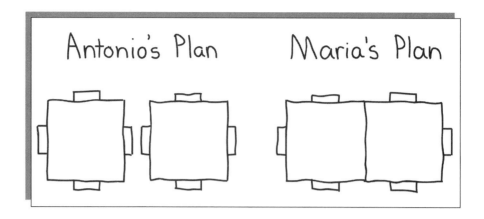

On chart paper, I sketched the two tables arranged both ways, to refer to later. As I was drawing, I asked the class questions that reassured me that they understood the situation and the drawing. I explained that Antonio and Maria's table problem would be the subject for today's math group work and that on another day we would write letters to tell Antonio and Maria our ideas for arranging the tables at their banquet.

I showed them two two-column charts, one for Antonio and one for Maria, on poster paper taped to the wall. I laughed and said, "Guess what? In math we sometimes call this a function *table*, but no one sits at it; we use it to keep numbers organized." I wrote "Two-Column Chart" and "Function Table" on my poster paper. "We'll write Number of Tables for the left column and Number of Seats for the right column. For example, with Antonio's way, if I put a 1 in the Tables column, how many seats can I have?" I did this for one and two tables on each of the charts. Then, I asked the students to work in groups for three minutes to talk about different numbers of tables and chairs for the charts. A few students chose to discuss the problem in their native Spanish language. I wanted to ensure that everyone understood the two-column chart and the situation.

Figure 3.2   The teacher modeled how to organize the students' answers in two-column charts.

Antonio's Plan   Maria's Plan

Number of Tables	Number of Seats		Number of Tables	Number of Seats
1	4		1	4
2	8		2	
3				

Two-Column Chart

Function Table

So, we briefly discussed their results orally, but didn't record their information because that would be their job during group work time. I told them I was confident that they could work together and solve the day's problem. Each group had color tiles and inch grid paper available for possible use. I gave the students copies of the Table Arrangement Problem and said, "This paper is for reference. Notice that it is notes about what we already talked about." We did choral reading of the problem statement. As the groups worked, I circulated and encouraged each group to use tiles to build table arrangements, or to sketch them, and to record their findings.

After the children had been working for about ten minutes, it was time for the groups to prepare to share. I wanted them to use the word *notice*. I wrote, "I noticed that . . ." on a piece of chart paper. "Now, each group should get ready to say three things that you noticed while working on this problem. For example, "I noticed that Antonio's plan starts with one table and four seats, but then has two and eight." After a few minutes, I asked for "a quiet hand" from someone who would share what they noticed. I called on Julia, and she told the class, "There were more Antonio's way." I then modeled, "Yes, you could say, 'I noticed that there were more seats Antonio's way.'" After echoing Julia's statement, I reminded the group to use the phrase "I noticed that . . ." I made sure that each group shared an observation and I also asked questions to help students extend their comments.

After the sharing, I asked them to make sure that each group member's paper had the drawings of the table arrangements, the labeled two-column charts with the numbers recorded, and (I hoped, depending upon their writing fluency) one or more sentences about what they noticed.

As they continued working, I asked questions of group members, "Why are there fewer places to sit when the tables touch? What happened when we acted it out with students and pretend tables? Why did Ricky and Mai have to move away from their tables? When you add a table to a long row, how many more seats do you gain?" I had planned these questions in advance because I wanted to get them to see that with Maria's plan, for every table added, only two seats are added. That, along with their sketches, would make it possible to work backward and think about the number of tables needed for 40 people. Next year the students would be ready to look at similar two-column charts and devise algebraic rules for the relationships.

During the last 10 minutes of the lesson, as an informal assessment, I asked the question, "How many people could sit at ten tables pushed together? How do you know?" By collecting work from each student, I was able to quickly glance through the papers and see where we needed to go next. I asked myself, "Are we ready to summarize our conclusions and write the letters to Antonio and Maria? Do we need to do more work on finding the rules for finding the number of seats when you know the number of tables? Do some students need help with the charts or the vocabulary?" I looked forward to the next lesson.

■ DISCUSSION OF THE MATHEMATICS TEACHING EXAMPLE

Notice that in this example, students not only gained experience with the mathematical concept, they also had several opportunities to extend their English language skills. Also, several techniques were used to support the involvement of all students. A copy of the teacher's lesson planning map and a planning map template are included in the Appendix as Exhibits A3.1 and A3.2.

Mathematics Goals

It appears that the teacher's mathematical goal goes well beyond this particular lesson to building a deep understanding and strong foundation in linear functions. The mathematical ideas in this lesson are usually new to fourth-grade students and are a very important foundation for understanding regular rate of change such as "two more seats for every extra table," and also how data tables, models, and diagrams can help uncover function rules. The focus on a problem-solving situation helps give meaning to functional relationships and to their representation in a function table. The questions about seating 40 people are quite challenging, but useful in leading students to begin to generalize about the relationship between the number of tables and the number of people.

This activity can be thought of as scaffolded problem solving—not true open-ended problem solving because, by asking for the use of sketches and two-column charts and by asking guiding questions, the teacher provided the beginning of an approach and other assistance. It is a good first step in providing access to grade-level problem solving for English learners.

Language Goals

The teacher was highlighting, and sometimes explicitly teaching, targeted language and vocabulary. Terms that were likely to be used during the lesson and in the future were modeled, explained, and written on the charts using examples from the problem context. During the class discussion, the phrase, "I noticed that . . ." was presented as a structure for responding, enabling English learners to prepare to share an observation and to stretch their spoken language skills.

Advance Organizers

In addition to helping students connect the problem situation to their personal experience and helping students comprehend the situation by acting out a portion of the problem, the teacher planned ahead a few key questions that might be asked and structured the problem statement to clearly communicate the assignment.

Creating Access to the Lesson

Notice that the problem statement is fairly wordy and complex. Instead of passing out the problem, the teacher launched the lesson orally by discussing a familiar situation and by introducing a "dilemma" for the students to solve for another class. This strategy helps actively involve all students in the lesson and sets a positive tone. An additional goal is to decrease students' anxiety (affective filter) about the learning at hand and the use of English.

The use of a variety of representations aided communication. Acting out the basic problem situation not only served to help everyone understand the problem situation, but also gave students direct experiences to speak about, and to reflect on, as they searched for mathematical relationships and rules.

Creating Support During the Lesson

The posters created during the initial part of the lesson offer an accessible visual reminder of ideas and of new academic terms, and they serve as a model of a graphic organizer that groups are expected to use. The copy of the problem serves as a written reminder of the most important parts of the assignment. The expectation of cooperative group work leads to increased attempts to use English to express ideas, to listen to others, and to understand the new mathematical ideas.

TEACHING TIPS   ■

- Draw attention to connections to prior experience and points of familiarity throughout a mathematics lesson.
- Help students use graphic organizers and develop practical diagrams and sketches to aid in thinking and in communicating with others.
- Help students use objects, including both manipulatives and people, as thinking and communication tools.
- State a clear question, purpose, and motivation for a lesson and help students remain focused around the question.
- Ask questions to help students sort out what they understand and what they need to understand next.
- Offer a classroom procedure that allows students to ask for "helpful hints" from another student or teacher without having the solution given away.
- Create and post sentence prompts (for example, "I want to find out . . ."; "I am sure this is correct because . . .") and encourage students to use them when solving problems and when discussing mathematics.
- Present challenging problems and learning tasks that require higher-order thinking skills, that promote communication, and that provide meaningful opportunities for scaffolding.
- Teach students how to listen to each other by having them restate other students' comments ("I heard George say, . . ."), by asking a question, or by adding their own idea ("I'd like to build on Lily's idea . . .").

Figure 3.3   Posters and other visual displays provide accessible scaffolding as new concepts, skills, and language are learned and become routine.

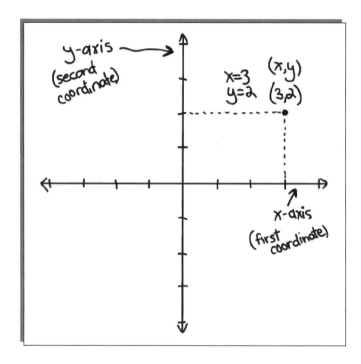

- Use a "think-aloud" format to demonstrate your own thought processes as you solve a problem and model the language and vocabulary that you expect students to use.

■ DISCUSSION OF SCAFFOLDING IN MATHEMATICS

Scaffolding refers to a specific type of coaching in which a teacher or other knowledgeable guide gives initial support for learning, with the goal of the development of students' independent learning skills. Scaffolding may take the form of a question that helps the student focus on pertinent information and thus make a decision on how to proceed next. It may involve a subtle hint, or a reminder of a similar problem. In mathematics, the important characteristic of scaffolding is that it is done "without reducing the complexity of the task at hand or specifying exactly how to proceed" (National Research Council, 2001, p. 336).

What is most important to realize is that through effective scaffolding, students can encounter more challenging questions and engage in higher-order thinking as they develop both important mathematical concepts and related language. Modifications may need to be made for oral or written responses, but all students with basic language skills can make significant mathematical progress when involved in a carefully scaffolded lesson. The mathematics teaching strategies selected by a teacher for a particular lesson may be determined by the content and by students' prior experience and knowledge, while the language objectives are determined by the teacher's knowledge of the existing levels of fluency of each of the students in the classroom (Chamot & O'Malley, 1994). But, while language fluency levels vary, they should not prevent each student from engaging in meaningful, challenging mathematics work.

Strategies that are of particular benefit to English learners include:

- Activating prior knowledge by first focusing on already understood concepts and skills
- Having frequent student-to-student interactions centered on mathematical ideas, including compelling real-world applications
- Having help in sorting out what is already understood and what to do next, and
- Regularly using visual, tactile, and auditory aids

The scaffolding of a mathematics lesson often begins by activating prior knowledge to assist students in moving from known information toward new understanding. This was seen in the lesson when the problem was acted out by children and then related data were posted on a two-column chart. Advance organizers that develop initial comprehension of the context, key ideas, and vocabulary for a particular mathematics lesson lead to equitable opportunities to learn. Through the use of visual aids and a few well-chosen questions, teachers can help students recognize the life knowledge and experience that they bring to a problem from outside mathematics. In addition, routines, classroom structures, and visual advance organizers can reduce the anxiety levels of English learners as they prepare for, and engage in, new learning.

How does cooperative group work provide scaffolding?

One purpose of cooperative group work is to provide frequent opportunities for students to speak about their ideas, to hear other students' ideas, and to ask questions. The discussion of ideas in itself often provides the necessary scaffolding for a student to get "unstuck" and to proceed with a mathematics problem. Another purpose is for group members to build on one another's understanding of new content.

Scaffolding toward language goals can occur during small-group work sessions. Groups are most productive when they are assisted in establishing equitable and respectful ways of interacting, and when members are motivated by the task at hand. Under such circumstances, each individual gains ideas from classmates and has frequent opportunities to ask questions and also to practice speaking to a few classmates.

As is seen in the lesson at the beginning of the chapter, each member of a cooperative group can be held accountable for specific outcomes. During cooperative group discussion in the lesson, the teacher communicated confidence and high expectations of each group's ability to help one another solve the problem. Asking questions, rather than showing solutions, is used to redirect and extend a group's focus. Finally, each student had his or her own problem page and was expected to record his or her thinking. Further scaffolding was provided through the instruction for group members to "make sure that each person had on their own paper" the expected outputs that were also clearly listed on the student handout. Informal assessment at the end of the lesson helps the student and teacher determine what was understood so far.

What are benefits of emphasizing problem solving in mathematics lessons for English learners?

When a lesson has a problem-solving focus, there are opportunities to build understanding from connections to prior problems and related mathematical concepts and skills, as well as from situations in everyday life. Well-chosen problems can have multiple entry points that allow students to get started in a variety of ways, rather than worrying about understanding the "right way" that is expected by the teacher. When a new concept or skill is studied in terms of a problem in context, there is more for students to discuss, thus offering increased opportunities to develop language skills. Also, when the context of a problem is understood, it can offer a bridge to prior knowledge and to understanding and remembering the new, abstract mathematical idea.

How is scaffolding of new mathematics concepts different from carefully planned direct instruction?

In some ways, this question is similar to the difference between *learning* and *acquisition* of a second language, or the difference between being taught procedures and developing concepts. Direct instruction can be used effectively to systematically show students a basic skill or procedure, such as how to fill out and read a table or chart. *Scaffolding* refers to instructional supports for more complex learning of a new mathematics concept or problem-solving strategy. For example, scaffolding a lesson on finding patterns and function rules can create the opportunity for students to identify, represent, compare, and discuss a number of patterns within a table of values. As was contended by Vygotsky (1978), the students are able to do more complex mathematics because of guiding questions and structure offered by the teacher. Scaffolding in mathematics is closer to coaching than to modeling and guiding; modeling isn't sufficient for developing independent learning skills (Gersten & Jiménez, 1998).

In a well-crafted, scaffolded lesson, there is evidence of purposeful use of teaching strategies and supports toward both the mathematics and language goals. The teacher involves students in active learning through gestures and demonstrations and supports the lesson by using visuals and concrete materials appropriate to the work at hand. However, the demonstrations are not so detailed as to reduce the challenge or interest level of the problem. The teacher does not give away solutions or answers and often encourages students to find multiple solution strategies. Students are expected to think about the problem or idea at hand and to develop solutions and ideas, both on their own and during group discussion. "There is growing evidence that students learn best when they are presented with academically challenging work that focuses on sense making and problem solving as well as skill building" (National Research Council, 2001).

Scaffolding involves helping students learn to reflect on their understanding of topics and processes; that is, supporting student engagement in metacognitive activity (Gersten & Jiménez, 1998). Such general habits can be supported through posted cues, such as "What do you need to find out?" "What do you already know?" "What does this remind you of?" and "Why do you think your solution is correct?" Generally, the teacher guides the lesson to closure with a clear summary of what the students have learned, what in particular should be remembered, and what should still be explored.

How is scaffolding used to support English language development during mathematics lessons?

Through the teacher's purposeful and repeated use of targeted academic language, coupled with related sense-making activities, students first become able to comprehend and later to use academic language. Frequent modeling and use of commonly used language structures (with accompanying posters) and teaching of exact words, phrases, and sentence frames are forms of language scaffolding. Teachers can also ask scaffolding questions to help students draw upon ideas and conversational language that they already know to expand their overall use of the target language.

Establishment of routines can scaffold language learning. For example, routines for class discussions, along with structured instructions, create a reason for students to rehearse something to say and offer a meaningful venue for speaking. A class might regularly be asked to "First think about the problem on your own. Then, after the signal, share with your neighbor. Please start by saying, 'I know that . . .' and use these three words on our list." In the teaching example, we saw this type of scaffolding when the teacher asked the students to say, "I noticed that. . . ."

Carefully structured small-group assignments increase students' opportunities to practice using new mathematical academic language and language in general. Frequent student-to-student discussions of mathematical ideas also make it possible for more advanced peers to offer support for mathematics learning.

The scaffolding of language enhances student opportunities for successful participation in classroom discussions and increases acquisition of both conversational and academic language.

SCAFFOLDING RESEARCH ■

There are many ways to scaffold lessons. Scaffolding may include, but is not limited to, the following strategies: verbal interaction, visible graphic organizers, cue lists, classroom routines, and other student-supportive strategies (Echevarria et al., 2004). This is compatible with the repertoire of instructional processes such as using multiple representations as tools that lead to understanding mathematics concepts (NCTM, 2000). Leinhardt (1988) emphasizes the importance of establishing routines and having predictable lesson segments to help students focus their learning efforts. Four basic types of routines—management, support, exchange, and learning—offer English learners a type of scaffolding. Routines invoke a shared known set of behaviors for moving through each lesson segment. These routines provide "the freedom necessary for fruitful intellectual exploration" (Leinhardt, 1988).

The scaffolding of learning of mathematics concepts involves many strategies similar to those used to support English language development.

However, in mathematics, scaffolding goes beyond strategies such as helping students become actively involved, think about what they already know, and recognize how the topic at hand is related to known ideas. Scaffolding includes helping students grapple with new mathematical ideas until they develop a new, firm understanding (Gersten & Jiménez, 1998). Through scaffolding, students are given opportunities to discover, confront, and rethink any misconceptions they may have about the ideas or methods they are learning (Idol, Jones, & Mayer, 1991).

One scaffolding technique is to guide students to more sophisticated understanding through interaction with a series of interrelated problems or ideas and related questioning. (See also Chapter 6, "Questioning Strategies," in this book.) Another technique, based on Vygotsky's theory, is to provide challenging tasks, with collaborative support, including considerable social interaction (National Research Council, 2001; Vygotsky, 1978). Schoenfeld (2002) brings attention to research that shows that in the course of being guided in the solution of a variety of well-chosen, meaningful, challenging problems, students not only become strong at problem solving, but their basic skills improve as well.

■ PRACTICE AND DISCUSSION QUESTIONS

1. What scaffolding techniques do you currently use when teaching mathematics? What techniques would you like to add to your teaching practice? Give examples.

2. Think about a recent lesson that you have taught (or plan for a future lesson) and the list of Teaching Tips in this chapter. What specifically would you do to enhance your lesson to scaffold mathematics and language learning for English learners?

3. Why is it advisable to use problem-solving situations when teaching mathematics to English learners? How do problem-solving situations allow for increased scaffolding?

4. Look back at the teaching example at the beginning of the chapter. How can you scaffold the directions to prepare children to write the best possible letter to Antonio and Maria?

5. Look at the lesson planning map in the Appendix, and name three or four ideas that you might add for your lesson planning. Explain the possible results.

4

The Role of Concrete Materials

Utilize Objects to Develop Mathematical Understanding for English Learners

RATIONALE FROM RESEARCH ■

Concrete materials are generally thought of as physical objects, and in some cases, movable objects on a computer screen, that aid learning (Terry, 1996). Although they are often used to assist students in understanding mathematical concepts, they are not *guaranteed* to produce learning. Clements remarks that "students may need concrete materials to build meaning initially, but they must reflect on their *actions* with manipulatives to do so. Later, they are expected to have a 'concrete' understanding that goes beyond these physical manipulatives" (Clements & McMillen, 1996, p. 271). Clements (1999) distinguishes between *sensory-concrete* knowledge, when students use sensory material to grasp an idea such as basic counting, and *integrated-concrete* knowledge, which is the result of developing connected knowledge. Sensory-concrete materials can aid in instruction that is designed to help students develop "interconnected knowledge," where the "physical objects, the actions they perform on the objects, and the abstractions they make all are interrelated in a strong mental structure" (Clements, 1999, p. 48).

When students use concrete materials in a meaningful way, the materials can serve as a vehicle to expanded understanding and ways of thinking about a concept and improve students' attitudes toward mathematics (Bustamante & Travis, 2005; Sowell, 1989). Concrete materials should enable students to explore and deepen new cognitive and mathematical structures as they work with a variety of tasks and questions. When English learners are exposed to multiple representations of a concept, including various concrete representations, they have increased access to verbal information and more opportunities to develop mental models and solid understanding.

Researchers have found that the use of manipulative materials, along with pictures, words, and symbols, is essential to the development of student understanding of operations and fraction concepts (Behr, Lesh, Post, & Silver, 1983). However, the use of materials is not sufficient to developing new mathematics concepts and skills. Teachers must facilitate students' development of meaning for materials and for actions with materials (Clements, 1999; Clements & McMillen, 1996; National Council of Teachers of Mathematics [NCTM], 2000).

■ MATHEMATICS TEACHING EXAMPLE

District Fifth-Grade Benchmark

Multiply by a Fraction

Work with your partner. Use counters as you solve these problems. Make up a short story and tell what real objects the counters stand for in each problem. Draw sketches to show your thinking.

A. $\frac{1}{3}$ of 6 = ___

B. $\frac{1}{3} \times 8 =$ ___

C. $\frac{3}{4}$ of 12

Two second-year, fifth-grade teachers collaborated to develop the following lesson plan as part of a professional development course on "Meeting the Needs of English Learners in the Mathematics Classroom." The instructor of the course asked that they plan a lesson on a significant new concept for a class with students of varied levels of English language proficiency. They were asked to include the use of concrete materials and to write out specific plans of what they will say, write, draw, and do during the delivery of the lesson. The teachers decided to focus on an initial lesson that would build toward success with the related fifth-grade district benchmark assessment items.

Goals:	Build concept and understanding of symbolic notation for finding a fractional part of a whole number	Rationale
Standard:	NS 2.4 Understand the concept of multiplication . . . of fractions	

LESSON STEPS

Introduction/Motivation Explain that we will work with counters, but "let's pretend that they are cookies." Show package of 15 cookies. Make connection to 15 counters that "stand for" cookies. Name Lupe as student-owner of the cookies and have students tell about Lupe's cookies—how they taste, look, smell, etc. Ask about sharing things like cookies, all agree that fair shares, equal amounts, are important.		Motivation; accessing and building prior experience; oral language opportunity Building meaning for manipulatives; modeling use of counters to stand for other objects
Step 1 **Do:**	Have two students pass out baggies of 15 counters to each student.	Active engagement
Say:	How many counters do you have in your bag? How many cookies do they stand for? "Put 15 counters on your desk. They stand for Lupe's 15 cookies. Divide them into 3 equal groups."	Instruction with emphasis on building meaning for fraction notation and relationship to division
Write:	$\frac{}{3}$ of 15 and connect to words "divide into 3 equal groups"	
Draw:	*not yet*	
Step 2 **Say:**	How many cookies or counters are there in 1 of the equal groups? (5) What about 2 equal groups? (10) 3 equal groups? (15, all of them) Refresh idea that thirds means three equal groups.	Guided practice
Write:	There were fifteen counters in a package. Two-thirds of them will be put in a box. How many counters will be put in a box?	Checking for understanding
Say:	Let's read this problem together. Is this like our problem with Lupe's cookies? Discuss with your group. (Yes, it's like she is planning to save $\frac{2}{3}$ of the cookies.)	
Draw:	Have students sketch a solution as a group.	
Do:	Choose two group's sketches to discuss with whole class. Emphasize three equal groups and hearing the fraction two-thirds. Explain that the *two* tells how many of those groups. (Don't write with fraction symbols yet.)	Practice making a sketch of a problem
Step 3 **Do:**	Show poster of these word problems; have monitors pass out copies to student. 1. One-third of the people in a family want mint chip ice cream. There are 6 people in the family. How many people want mint chip ice cream? 2. Three friends buy 8 chocolate brownies to share equally. How many brownies does each friend get? 3. Eight friends ordered burritos for lunch. One-fourth wanted beef burritos. How many wanted beef burritos? 4. Roberto has 16 gummy worms. He lets his four friends share them equally. How many gummy worms does each friend get?	Instruction

(Continued)

Figure 4.1   This student's drawing shows one way to arrange counters and "put two-thirds of 15 in a box."

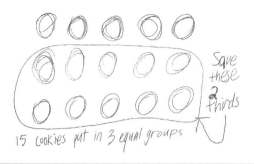

(Continued)		
Say:	Let's read the first problem together. Is this like our problem with Lupe's cookies? Discuss with your group. Who will tell us what your group thinks? Is this like our problem with Lupe's counters? (Alike because the denominator is 3; think of 3 equal groups; you need to find thirds. Different because you start with just 6, you aren't sharing, and in the earlier problem you need to find *two* thirds)	Modeling by students and teacher Students verbalize and hear idea
Write:	(Point to poster as students discuss problems; write symbolic problem to model recording as students tell about the problem, but primarily emphasize manipulative work)	Modeling use of symbols
Draw:	Students sketch a solution in their groups.	
Do:	Choose two groups' sketches to discuss with whole class.	
Step 4 **Say:**	On this paper there are three more problems. Now, work with just one partner. Read and talk about Problem 2. Use your counters and other methods to start to figure out this problem about chocolate brownies (clarify). After **four minutes** we will finish working on the problem all together.	Directions
Do:	Observe students and their discussions. Ask questions to guide and clarify. Encourage pretending counters are brownies. Note who recognizes a difficulty using counters for this problem. (8 isn't divisible by 3; can't break counters to share them)	Scaffolding Observing progress Preparing for class discussion
Say:	Let's work on this problem together. Everyone, show me on your fingers how many counters you used to model Problem 2. (8) How many equal groups did you need to make? Who can explain why three groups?	Guided practice
Write:	$\frac{-}{3}$ of 8 and connect to words "divide into 3 equal groups"	Modeling use of symbols
Say:	How many whole brownies does each friend get? What can we do with the other two? Yes, share the extra two brownies for the three friends. We can't cut our extra two plastic counters to share them! Please draw the extra two brownies and use lines to show how to cut them to divide them equally among the three friends. Look at my share; I get two brownies and one-third of this whole brownie plus one-third of this brownie. That gives me two and two-thirds brownies. Now, quickly make a picture of finding my share of one-third of eight brownies.	Extending thinking Guiding drawing of models
Draw:	All partner pairs draw on paper. Have two students draw on an overhead (OH) transparency, then share with whole class.	

Figure 4.2   One common method used by students to find $\frac{1}{3}$ of 8 brownies, or an equal share of 8 brownies for 1 of 3 people, is illustrated in this student work.

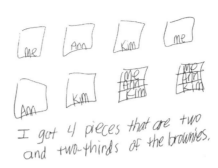

I got 4 pieces that are two and two-thirds of the brownies.

Do:	Have students share solutions. Make comments that connect problem, counters, and drawings. Show numerator 2 in fraction notation as naming the number of thirds. Make sure $\frac{2}{3}$ in the answer refers to" $\frac{2}{3}$ of a brownie."	
Say:	We just solved this problem: one-third of 8 = ___. How much is *one* third of eight? How much for one of the friends?	
Step 5		
Say:	You will have ten minutes to do the other two practice problems.	
Write:	Do the other two problems with your partner. Use counters. Draw to show your thinking.	Independent practice
Draw:	All partner pairs draw on paper. Have two students draw on an OH transparency to share with whole class.	Formative assessment
Do:	Have students share. Make comments that connect problem, counters, and drawings. Model fraction notation. Collect students' papers.	
Say:	If you and your partner finish early, think about this problem that we will discuss later this week: $\frac{1}{9}$ of 5 = ___ .	Extending understanding
Step 6		
(Watch the clock. Skip to Step 8 the last 5 minutes of the lesson.)		
Say:	Tomorrow we will write some more problems. Let's practice now. Find two-fifths of fifteen. This makes me think of a problem about fifteen things and two out of every five of the things are alike in some way.	Think-aloud (modeling)
Write:	There are 15 _____s. The _____s are put into _____ equal groups. $\frac{}{5}$ of the _____ are _____. How many _____ s are _____?	Prewriting; modeling of problem creation
Say:	In my mind, I think: There are fifteen carrots shared equally by five friends. The two boys eat theirs, the girls save theirs; two-fifths of the people eat their carrots right away. How many carrots are eaten?	
Draw:	5 stick figures, each with a bag. Model equal shares of the 15 items, then circle 2 parts to show the carrots eaten by the boys.	Modeling
Do:	Have partners discuss other possible scenarios before helping one student fill in the blanks.	Guided practice

(Continued)

(Continued)		
Step 7 **Say:** With your partner talk and invent another problem that asks about a fractional amount of a group of sixteen things. Use your red and yellow counters to model the problem. Hint: Be ready to say what fraction of the things is shown with red counters. **Write:** Talk and invent another problem. Write a first draft of your problem. **Draw:** Students represent their problem's solution on paper. **Do:** Call this a "first draft" and collect to read later.	Prewriting; making connections, generalizing about fractional parts Formative assessment	
Step 8 **Say:** Who will summarize about the type of problems that we did today? (Finding a fractional part of a group of things) What is a helpful way to think about the denominator, the bottom number, in these problems? (It tells how many groups to divide the things into) **Write:** Who will summarize about today? What is a helpful way to think about $\frac{1}{3}$ of 15 (think about 15 things, put into 3 equal-sized groups) **Do:** Have students count their 15 counters and zip their bags. Have two student "materials managers" collect the bags.	Closure	

■ DISCUSSION OF THE MATHEMATICS TEACHING EXAMPLE

Mathematics Goals

Prior to formal work multiplying by a fraction, the teacher addresses the main goal of making sense of finding a fractional amount of a whole number and also of related symbolic recordings. They begin with the simple problem of finding $\frac{1}{3}$ of 15 objects, then builds on that to find $\frac{2}{3}$ and also $\frac{3}{3}$ of 15 objects. This expands students' understanding of a useful interpretation of denominators, numerators, and given whole numbers.

A second goal is to develop general understanding of the denominator as a divisor and to make connections to prior experience making equal groups. Problems where the given whole number is not divisible by the denominator are also included.

Students gain awareness that problems with various contexts can be modeled in similar ways, beginning with a focus on "sharing" situations. The first and third word problems do not involve sharing, but do provide an opportunity to model the use of equal groups and fraction language to describe other situations. The initial use of objects helps students visualize the operation of division and deepen their understanding of quotients, especially when the numbers do not divide evenly.

The lesson appears to include a goal of helping students have multiple ways of thinking about future problems, including more complicated problems that are not easily solved with manipulatives.

Language Goals

The teachers intersperse the lesson with several mini–language lessons. The students are encouraged to read problems, help write a word problem, listen to the teacher and classmates, and speak. Using concrete materials supports the language goals because there is something tangible to read, write, listen to, and speak about. By using objects, the students' language can refer to concrete, visible objects such as cookies and counters. Vocabulary such as *stand for* and *represent* are made accessible in a mathematics context. The students are encouraged to discuss the posted problems and to identify connections between problems. Language is used to carefully build meaning for mathematical relationships. Finally, the written fraction equations are introduced in connection to language used with earlier problems.

Building Understanding by Using Concrete Materials

The teachers plan several direct contact experiences with objects. Also students can show their ideas and watch others work with objects, making content more accessible to English learners whenever verbal input is not comprehensible. The teacher realizes that the small plastic counters are not inherently meaningful. They plan to purposefully develop and reinforce the idea of having one object, such as a small round counter, represent some real-life, meaningful object, such as one of Lupe's cookies, or a brownie.

Partner and whole-class discussions are structured so that concrete objects can be seen and referred to in mathematical discussions. The teachers have students work with "real" problems (for example, sharing cookies) in order to create a link among the situation, the concrete objects, and the abstract mathematical operations. For example, division by the divisor is connected with the familiar experience of sharing equally and is modeled with counters and drawings.

Expanding Understanding Through Multiple Representations

The teachers plan to scaffold the concept of finding a fractional part of a whole number by including work with concrete materials, visual representations, written problems, and oral discussion. In addition to purposefully working with counters, students will make and discuss drawings that represent the brownie-sharing situation. They have an opportunity to grapple with the task of sharing 2 brownies with 3 children, and see that a drawing is helpful. Ideally, they would use gestures and words to connect cutting a brownie into 3 parts with lines drawn on a picture.

Verbal phrases are also a form of representation. A teacher could say, "I have fifteen things, divided into three equal groups, and I want to show how many are in two of those three equal groups." By connecting verbalization to concrete materials, and then to drawings and equations, students' understanding of the mathematics is expanded and their language skills develop at the same time.

Preplanning Key Lessons

The teachers have written out a detailed lesson plan, almost like a film script, with repeated exposure to essential ideas and with awareness of possible confusing aspects of finding fractional amounts. By carefully preselecting the problems to discuss and preparing some of the questions, a teacher is more likely to provide instruction that will make the mathematics content accessible to all students. Also materials management is carefully planned, thus minimizing interruptions to learning.

It would be interesting to hear the teachers' reasons for presenting a difficult second problem in this initial lesson and not giving students independent practice with such problems.

■ TEACHING TIPS

- Establish and practice routines for storing, retrieving, and sharing the various concrete materials in the classroom.
- When introducing a new manipulative aid, allow students a few minutes for free exploration with the materials to let them experiment and increase their curiosity.
- Emphasize to students that concrete materials are tools for thinking, for solving problems, and for communicating mathematical ideas and not for mimicking other people's thinking.

Figure 4.3   Students can learn about equivalent fractions and common denominators while folding their own set of paper fraction strips.

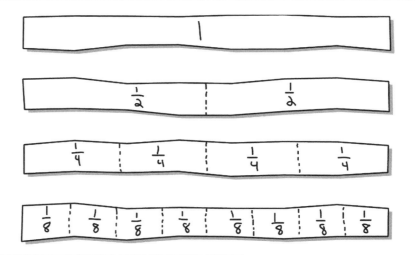

- Use a variety of concrete materials after developing a new concept or procedure with an initial manipulative material. For example, when developing fraction concepts over time, a class may fold paper, use linking cubes, draw pictures, work with sets of small objects, and discuss rulers.
- Help students analyze the benefits and drawbacks of various materials for particular problems.

- Ask students for suggestions of materials that they could bring from home to give more meaning to a new mathematics idea.
- Give students permanently connected objects, such as base-ten blocks and Cuisenaire rods, and also objects that students can connect and disconnect, such as linking cubes, to model numbers and operations.
- Explore computer-based virtual manipulatives and applets that are available online from curriculum publishers and on many other Web sites.
- Help students think about appropriate times to use concrete materials, as opposed to mental math, equations, and paper-pencil calculations.
- Use materials such as liquid measuring pitchers and rulers to help relate number and measurement.
- Do not expect students to learn primarily by watching the teacher manipulate concrete materials.
- Select manipulative materials that allow students to develop meaning by imposing their own understanding and ways of organizing the materials.

Figure 4.4   Manipulative materials can help students solve and discuss complex problems, as seen in this Grade 7 group report on their study of adding consecutive integers.

DISCUSSION OF CONCRETE MATERIALS IN MATHEMATICS ■

It is important for students to be *actively* using materials to investigate mathematical ideas. It is not sufficient for students to use manipulative materials during mathematics lessons in which the teacher does most of the talking and thinking. For example, students are more likely to develop an understanding of area if they work with square tiles to estimate the number of tiles needed to cover the "floor" of an empty box. Explaining their work through words, pictures, diagrams, or mathematical symbols is another aspect of ensuring that work with materials is actually developing the intended mathematical ideas.

During the "guided practice" phase of a lesson, the teacher's role is to help students connect the objects that they are using to the mathematics and to related vocabulary. This type of work does not lead to skill immediately, but requires that students repeatedly use the concrete materials in a variety of contexts to gain familiarity, fluency, and ultimately, to connect the models to their own unique way of understanding. When students can use a manipulative to show a concept, they are motivated by the new knowledge that they can create and demonstrate.

When is it appropriate to use concrete materials in the mathematics classroom?

Concrete materials give access to new mathematical concepts to many students who might otherwise struggle. When used correctly, they can help every student, at any age, focus on a lesson and think more deeply about the ideas that are being studied. Concrete materials are a particularly crucial part of the instruction of fluency among Level 1 and 2 English learners. This is because materials help students focus on new concepts and relevant vocabulary at the same time. For example, imagine how hard it would be to teach third graders (with any level of language proficiency) about hundreds and thousands without actually having ten hundred objects or related models. Not only can the phrase and quantity *one hundred* be given meaning through tactile and visual experience, but the relationship between ten hundreds and one thousand can be emphasized.

Similarly, paper rectangles can be manipulated when teaching topics such as multiplying fractions. One common method is to start with a rectangle that represents the whole unit, then folding and cross-hatching to show three-fourths of the unit and finally folding and cross-hatching in the other direction to find one-half of three-fourths. Or, a transparent yellow half-rectangle can be laid over a transparent blue three-fourths-rectangle, to find out what fraction of the whole rectangle turns green because it is one-half of three-fourths and also three-fourths of one-half.

Figure 4.5   A common diagram for multiplying $\frac{1}{2} \times \frac{3}{4}$. First show three-fourths of a unit rectangle, then find one-half of that amount.

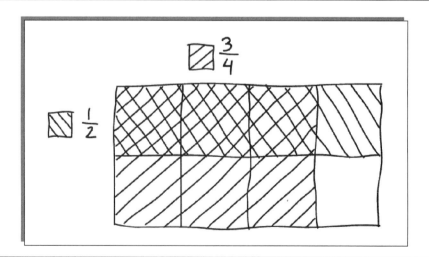

What should teachers be aware of when using concrete materials?

Concrete representations are most effectively used when the purpose is to expand students' conceptual understanding of a mathematical idea. It is important to have clear goals in mind about the specific ideas that will be discussed by the end of a lesson. On the other hand, it is often problematic to use concrete representations primarily for the purpose of demonstrating a calculation procedure. In such cases, manipulatives or other representations may not be tied to meaning for many students, resulting in attempts to mimic the teacher's actions without mathematical understanding. For example, many students have been discovered to have very little place value sense and understanding of larger numbers, in spite of working with "hundreds," "tens," and "ones" base-ten blocks. Instead, they see a number such as 314 written on a place value chart as a simple recipe to "get 3 big squares, 1 long stick, and 4 units."

In spite of what a teacher says or demonstrates, each student makes his or her own interpretation of the meaning of work with concrete representations. For example, when using objects to show the fraction $\frac{5}{8}$, some students will explain that all you need to do is "Get eight things because of the bottom number, but make sure that five of the things are all alike because of the top number," while others may focus on having a unit, or whole set, where 5 out of every 8 parts are somehow special. It is up to the teacher to build connections between a model, the underlying concept, and common written and spoken forms of a mathematical idea.

Is the concrete-pictorial-abstract sequence still promoted?

Lesh and others have stressed that developing integrated-concrete understanding requires a more complex model than a linear concrete-pictorial-abstract sequence (Behr et al., 1983). Students deepen their understanding as they become aware of connections and switch, in any order, among real-world situations, manipulative aids, pictures, and spoken and written symbols. A topic or lesson may start from any of these five points of view, with connections to other representations subsequently carefully developed. Work with objects might be preceded by a story or an experience with a real-world situation, as was seen in this chapter's teaching example. Shared meaning may be developed around work with movable objects, connected to drawing diagrams to represent work with objects, and then related to mathematical symbols to stand for such work. Also, as students develop and practice a concept, they may be given an equation and asked to invent a story to match. Such varied experiences develop connections that lead from students' initial informal understanding to integrated-concrete knowledge and versatility in use of the concept or skill.

Also teachers should be aware of the differences between work with concrete objects that can be handled and moved and semi-concrete representations, such as pictures, that are static and require mental analysis or manipulation. Neither necessarily communicates a teacher's intended meaning. While the abstract or symbolic form of mathematical representation is accepted as needing careful teaching, concrete and semi-concrete representations also need purposeful discussion in order to promote productive interpretations by students.

■ CONCRETE MATERIALS RESEARCH

In a discussion of the NCTM Process Standards, the Annenberg Teaching Math online site (WGBH Educational Foundation, 2003) explains that "mathematical representation" refers to the wide variety of ways to capture an abstract mathematical concept or relationship. A mathematical representation may be visible, such as a number sentence, a display of manipulative materials, or a graph, but it may also be an internal way of seeing and thinking about a mathematical idea. Regardless of their form, representations can enhance students' communication, reasoning, and problem-solving abilities; help them make connections among ideas; and aid them in learning new concepts and procedures. Concrete materials are the tangible elements in this set of ways to facilitate powerful learning.

"Representations do not 'show' the mathematics to the students. Rather, the students need to work with each representation extensively in many contexts as well as move between representations in order to understand how they can use a representation to model mathematical ideas and relationships" (NCTM, 2000, p. 208). Once a concept has been demonstrated and explored using a first manipulative, work with other manipulatives can lead to children's considerations of how the new manipulative represents the targeted concept, and ultimately lead to more generalized understanding (Behr et al., 1983).

The goal of instruction should be to help students develop mathematical proficiency, including deep, connected knowledge that can be applied purposefully in varied situations (NCTM, 2000; National Research Council, 2001). When students move and arrange manipulative materials, they gain kinesthetic input and develop an additional path for recalling ideas. When tactile and visual learning are significant meaning-centered components of instruction, benefits include not only increased access to ideas, but also multiple ways of thinking and communicating about the ideas.

Concrete materials do not always lead to greater learning. When careful attention is not paid to fostering students' development of meaning for objects, when a teacher tutors students to use materials in a prescribed step-by-step way, surprising misconceptions can develop (Clements, 1999; Clements & McMillen, 1996; Thompson, 1994). Manipulative materials, such as linking cubes, square tiles, or base-ten blocks, have the potential of helping both teachers and students communicate mathematical ideas. However, it is quite possible for students to simply mimic the teacher's use of manipulatives in a rote manner and to misapply learned procedures. Manipulatives should not add a layer of complexity or frustration to learning, but rather should help students actively engage in developing meaning for mathematics (Moyer, 2001; Weiss, 2006). Clements reminds us that "although manipulatives have an important place in learning, they do not carry the meaning of the mathematical idea" (Clements & McMillen, 1996, p. 253).

Concrete materials are also important to vocabulary and general language development. For example, consider the importance of having something for each student to touch when building meaning for words and phrases such as *edge, corner, to fold,* and *to rotate.* "Relating new vocabulary to tangible objects is one of the basic premises of second-language instruction. Words are easier to remember when students can see and touch the objects they represent while repeatedly hearing and saying the new words" (Garrison & Mora, 2005, p. 41). Interestingly, Garrison and Mora point out that once a concept "has been established, students do not need to relearn the concept in English"; they need only to learn the English label for the previously established concept. Therefore, vocabulary must be learned in each new language; concepts, once mastered, do not need to be retaught, but merely refreshed and connected to new words (Cummins, 1984). Of course, concrete materials can facilitate the learning and remembering of new vocabulary in a new language.

PRACTICE AND DISCUSSION QUESTIONS ■

1. Think about a lesson that involves manipulative materials. What would you say and do to make sure that students understand the mathematics and are not just moving the materials?

2. In the teaching example in this chapter, mathematics manipulatives and sketches of objects are used both as (1) an initial aid to instruction for skill development that can be set aside when they are no longer needed by a student, and (2) as a way of providing multiple models to help develop and expand students' understanding of a concept. Give examples of each strategy from the teaching example. Apply these two approaches to your own teaching and describe how you might use manipulatives in both ways.

3. What specific changes in the use of concrete materials are you considering making in your classroom? Give detailed examples.

4. What are some possible problems associated with the use of manipulatives with English learners?

5

Visual Learning

Provide Mathematical and Organizational Representations as a Regular Component of Instruction

RATIONALE FROM RESEARCH ■

Traditionally, teachers teach by talking—they rely heavily on linguistic input in the form of spoken and written language when presenting new information to students. However, research has shown that assisting students in generating *nonlinguistic* representations for new knowledge not only aids thinking, communication, and recall, but also stimulates and increases activity in the brain (Gerlic & Jausovec, 1999; Marzano, Norford, Paynter, Pickering, & Gaddy, 2001). For English learners, it is essential that communication tools go beyond the spoken and written word. In mathematics class, visual tools such as graphic organizers and diagrams offer visual means of communicating information and thinking about mathematical relationships. In any class setting, visual tools help students develop conceptual understanding while they compare and contrast representations and solution methods (National Research Council, 2001).

A variety of visual representations are seen In the excerpts and commentary of the following lesson.

■ MATHEMATICS TEACHING EXAMPLE

Two-Digit Multiplication

> **Problem of the Day: How Many Chairs?**
>
> Chairs need to be set up in the multipurpose room for an assembly.
> In this room, 23 rows of chairs will fit.
> In each row, 34 chairs will fit.
> How many chairs will fit in the room?
> Show how you know in at least two ways.

Several fourth-grade teachers were talking about mathematics during their grade-level meeting. They were discussing how they were going to introduce two-digit multiplication this year. First, they reflected on last year's difficulties, remarking that some students:

Figure 5.1
A common student error when multiplying two-digit numbers with the standard algorithm.

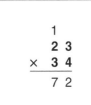

- Often forgot the steps when multiplying (Figure 5.1)
- Didn't know the multiplication facts
- Couldn't easily multiply numbers such as 30 times 40
- Couldn't visualize larger numbers
- Didn't realize that the product of two two-digit numbers must be a large number, an answer in the hundreds or thousands

In discussing their plan for the current year, they decided to include in their lessons:

- Work with manipulatives
- Problems in context
- Group work
- Student-drawn diagrams
- Class discussions of students' methods

At their biweekly meeting, the teachers agreed to include the Problem of the Day: How Many Chairs? in their plans to teach two-digit multiplication and to look at student work at their next meeting. Excerpts from some of Ms. Walker's lessons during the next two weeks follow.

Ms. Walker's first lesson begins with a warm-up (Figure 5.2) that reviews previous learning and continues with the Problem of the Day.

Ms. Walker: As you do Part A on your warm-up sheet right now, you may want to look at our wall posters to remind yourself of our other work with arrays. If you get stuck, talk to your neighbor.

MS. WALKER: Now, what is this warm-up problem about? Tell me what you drew.

STUDENTS: Arrays. Eight teams . . . Six on each team. Six in every row . . .

MS. WALKER: Remember, arrays can be used to show different kinds of multiplication problems. Talk to your neighbor about your array. For example, I noticed that some people drew an array with 6 dots across and some drew it with 8 across [gesturing]. Explain how to see the teams in your array. . . . Now, work with your neighbor on Number 8 in your warm-up. I will listen as you talk about your ways to break the array into two parts to find the total . . . .

MS. WALKER: Let's all work together to write number sentences and words that tell about Karina's way to break the array into two parts to find the total (Figure 5.3). What shall we write? . . .

MS. WALKER: Today, thinking about rows and arrays may help us. We'll be working on another problem, but with much bigger numbers. Picture in your mind our multipurpose room, with lots of rows of chairs. I'm going to tell you a story about a room that's bigger than that at another school. At that school, they never figured out how many chairs could fit in their multipurpose room. [Ms. Walker draws on the board a school and several children's faces (Figure 5.4). Then she writes, "How many fit?" She continues to add to the drawing as she describes the situation.] They knew there could be 23 rows with 34 chairs in each row. Our job is to figure out how many chairs there will be.

Figure 5.2 A worksheet created as an advance organizer for students.

Warm-Up

Using Arrays to Model Multiplication

There are 8 teams. There are 6 children on each team.

Part A:

1. Show how to use an array to model this situation.
2. Write numbers next to the array to show what the array means.
3. What does the 6 stand for? _____ Write a label.
4. What does the 8 stand for? _____ Write a label.
5. Write these vocabulary words next to your array to help show what they mean.
   - Rows
   - Groups
   - Factor
   - Columns
   - Number in each group
   - Product
6. One student said, "This problem is easy because you just add 8 plus 6 to get the answer." This is not correct. Why don't you add eight plus six? What do you do with 8 and 6 in this problem?
7. What are some ways to find out the total number of children on the teams?

Part B:

8. Draw the array again. Draw a horizontal or vertical line to cut your array into two small arrays. Show how to use the two small arrays to find the total.

Figure 5.3 Karina's answer to Part B on the warm-up, with the class's suggestions for number sentences to describe her work.

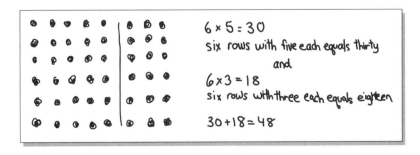

Figure 5.4   Figures drawn by Ms. Walker as she was explaining the task.

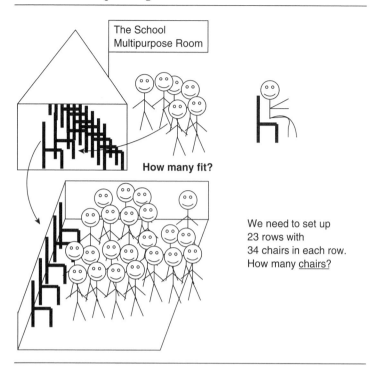

The School Multipurpose Room

How many fit?

We need to set up
23 rows with
34 chairs in each row.
How many <u>chairs</u>?

MS. WALKER: We're going to learn many ways to solve problems like this today and in the next few days. Remember, last week we skip-counted by fives to figure out an answer. For these numbers it might be too hard to count by thirty-fours, right? So what should we do? What materials could we use to help?

[Ms. Walker guides the class in reading the Problem of the Day on the paper that is passed out. She points out that the problem asks for the total number of chairs and it asks for multiple ways to show the answer, so both are important to the task.]

MS. WALKER: Now turn to your neighbor and talk quickly about what you might do to figure out how many chairs there are in all. Then, we'll make a list of the ways you come up with.

MS. WALKER: Okay, please tell us one way that we can find the total number of chairs. [Ms. Walker makes a list while she calls on students.]

JOSÉ: Draw the rows and count them.

ALICIA: We said make tally marks.

ROBERTO: Base-ten blocks can show the rows, too.

MICHELLE: We can use the graph paper to draw the room and fill in the squares.

MS. WALKER: Does anyone have a way to use our square tiles?

ALANA: We can get the tiles and pretend that they are chairs and put them in rows like an array.

MS. WALKER: Okay, I'll come around and ask each group to try a different way from our list. Everyone at the table must help draw a diagram showing what their group does. Help one another. Then, we'll all look at your drawings and talk. I'll collect each group's paper at the end and we'll go on from there tomorrow. . . .

* * *

While some groups relied on repeated addition and acting out the problem, the following groups used visual strategies during their work:

Conversation at Group 1

ROBERTO: I got the base-ten blocks.

JAMAL: Put 'em in rows like the chairs. Make thirty-four in every row.

KARINA: I count them, thirty-four. [Starts counting out the units.]

JAMAL: No, put the tens down too.

KARINA: Chairs. [Points to the units.]

ARICELA: But you can put down a ten for ten chairs. It's faster. See, one, two, three, four, five, six, seven, eight, nine, ten chairs. [Counts the units on one ten block.]

ROBERTO: We need more. [Scoops up more tens and ones out of the tub.]

[All the children help put the tens and ones down to make rows of 34. They continue to talk while they work.]

ARICELA: [Stops putting down blocks and starts counting.] Ten, twenty, thirty, forty, fifty . . . two hundred forty. I can't finish; it's too many.

JAMAL: I'll count the ones.

* * *

Conversation at Group 2

JARED: I get to be the paper passer. I'll get the graph paper. . . .

VERONICA: Okay, I can draw it. [She counts only 30 squares across the paper.] Look, it makes too long a row. We need to tape it.

JARED: Here's more paper.

MIRANDA: I get tape.

JARED: Draw it all the way.

MIRANDA: How many chairs?

MARCOS: Thirty-four. Did you count the squares, Veronica?

JARED: We all have to draw it. Why are you drawing a line through the squares?

VERONICA: I'm showing each row. This is only Row 1.

(See Figure 5.5.)

* * *

Conversation at Group 3

DANTE: Here are the tiles. Let's line them up for rows of chairs.

VICTOR: How many we have to do?

OLIVIA: Push them all together so they're neat. Don't let them fall on the floor, Victor!

MONICA: We have to make twenty-three rows.

OLIVIA: You can't just make rows.

MONICA: How many were in each row?

DANTE: I think, thirty-four.

VICTOR: I have three rows!

Figure 5.5   Group 2's drawing on grid paper.

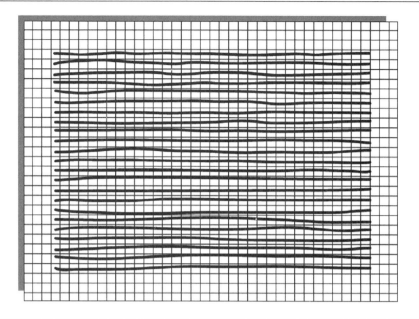

| OLIVIA: | We're not going to have enough! |
| DANTE: | I'll get more. |

* * *

MONICA:	Count it. [Starts counting in each row]
OLIVIA:	I'll count it too.
DANTE:	Be quiet, I'm counting them. Thirty-four, thirty-five, thirty-six, thirty-seven. . . . Wait, we can add it up. Get a calculator!
OLIVIA:	Uh oh! Time's up. We didn't finish counting and we didn't make drawings!

Conversation at Group 4

MARICELA:	Do tallies.
CIERRA:	I like tallies. It's easy.
RICHIE:	How many chairs were there?
SHANELLE:	Thirty-four.
CIERRA:	Okay, I'll make tallies. . . .
RICHIE:	But you have to do it again.
MARICELA:	Why?
SHANELLE:	We have to keep doing it—not just one time. That's just the front row. Keep going. Make thirty-four more.
MARICELA:	My turn. [She makes 34 more tallies.] We're all supposed to write it.
SHANELLE:	I'll count the rows until we get to twenty-three rows.

* * *

MARICELA: There is too many of tallies.

Ms. WALKER: Class, I know you're not all finished, but let's stop and show our diagrams and report on what we think about our methods so far.

During their reports, the tally group complains that it's "too many" and "confusing." The tiles group says, "It takes so long and we needed so many tiles," and "We didn't finish." The base-ten block group announces that "it got easier when we used the tens and not just the ones, but we ran out of tens and had to borrow some!" The grid paper group explains, "We traced across through thirty-four squares to make each row" [shown in Figure 5.5]. Ms. Walker has everyone stand up and look carefully at Group 1's and Group 3's base-ten block and tile representations so they can remember them, even after they clean up.

The next day, Ms. Walker begins by showing one student's labeled array from the previous day's warm-up problem. She briefly shows and then posts a diagram of Group 1's base-ten blocks and reminds students of the problem situation (shown in Figure 5.6). She then suggests that since Group 3 didn't have enough time to solve the problem using the tiles, everyone will help draw a diagram of the rows of square tiles that they looked at yesterday. She passes out quarter-inch grid paper and has students imagine that each grid square is a square tile. She models on the overhead as she guides the class in outlining and labeling a 23-by-34 rectangle. She begins by making 23 dots in a vertical column near the left side of her grid to start the rows. Next, she has the students count across to make sure there are 34 squares in each row. The result is a large 23- by-34 rectangle. Students in Group 2 notice the similarity to their grid paper diagram of the previous day.

Figure 5.6   A diagram created by the teacher to represent Group 1's base-ten block solution to the chairs problem.

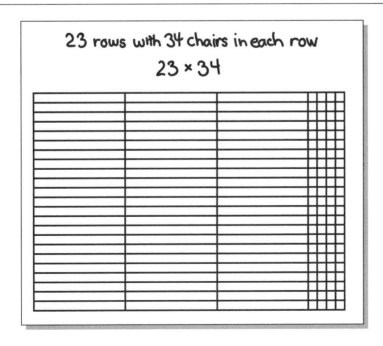

Ms. Walker: Hmm. How is your new diagram alike and different from Group 1's diagram of their base-ten block solution to the chairs problem?

Students: They used tens blocks. Both have twenty-three rows . . .

Ms. Walker: We still haven't had a chance to figure out how many chairs yet. Today we're going to see how base-ten block diagrams can help us find the total for big problems like this one. When students multiply to do this kind of problem, they sometimes forget to do all the parts of a problem. So we're going to learn about a way that helps us find the correct product, the answer. On the overhead I've put my drawing of Group 1's base-ten blocks [Figure 5.6]. Altogether, let's count the chairs represented by the tens over here. [All count, "10, 20, 30, 40, 50, 60, 70, 80, 90, 100!!"] Who will show a base-ten block that we can use here instead of these ten tens? [Ms. Walker calls on Victor, who offers to get a hundreds flat.]

Victor: [Shows the hundreds flat.] Ten tens same as hundred.

Ms. Walker: Roberto, would you like to come up and change my drawing to show where we can put Victor's hundred? [Roberto draws a square outline around the 100 chairs in the top, left corner. With guidance, he makes a total of 6 hundred-squares over a 20 by 30 area.]

Ms. Walker: Cierra, please come up and place my special little overhead hundreds-blocks on top of each of Roberto's hundreds? [Figure 5.7]

Ms. Walker: About how many chairs are there? Explain your estimate to your neighbor.

* * *

Figure 5.7   A base-ten block diagram showing hundreds in place of ten tens. Notice that students could exchange some ones for tens at the right of the diagram.

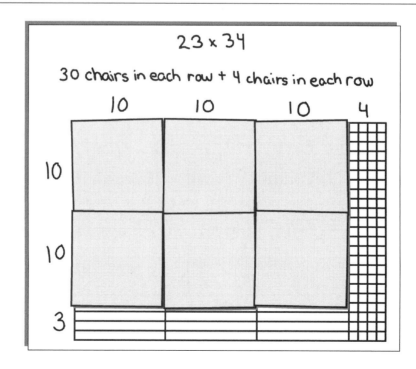

Ms. Walker: I heard many good estimates and explanations. I heard: "There are more than six hundred chairs because there are six areas, six sections with one hundred chairs each and still more chairs! Do you see that twenty rows with thirty chairs each is six hundred?

The class continues to figure out the number of chairs represented by the tens blocks and also by the ones blocks. Ms. Walker informally records the subtotals on the board and then the class adds to find the total, 782.

Over the next few days, Ms. Walker's class continues to work with rectangular diagrams for a variety of problems. The students see that it is often helpful to think of sections within an array. Some sections are easiest to represent with hundreds blocks, some by tens, and some by ones.

In preparation for upcoming work with algorithms for two-digit multiplication, Ms. Walker goes on to show how each section within the large rectangle stands for part of the multiplication problem 23 times 34 and is a "partial product" (Figure 5.8). She also helps the class see that this method can be applied to all two-digit multiplication problems.

Figure 5.8   Visual connections can be made between a rectangular diagram, a base-ten block model, and "partial products."

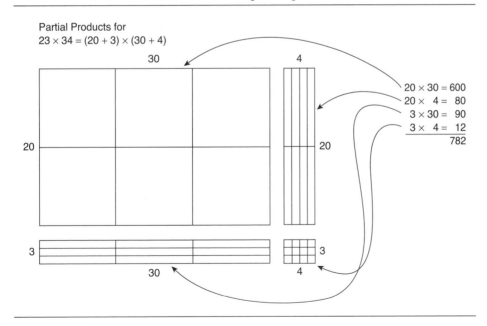

As the lessons continue, Ms. Walker sometimes gives students a new two-digit multiplication problem and asks them to model and solve it with a rectangular diagram. At other times, she shows a diagram of a finished rectangular model with lines separating the partial products and asks students to figure out and explain the dimensions and totals for each of the partial products. Gradually, they begin to record their work vertically as is shown in Figure 5.9. Ms. Walker reports that in the future she will model the use of a generic rectangular diagram to use as a graphic organizer for multiplying (Figure 5.10).

Figure 5.9   An alternative algorithm for multiplying two-digit numbers provides visual scaffolding.

$$
\begin{aligned}
34 &= 30 + 4 \\
\times\, 23 &= 20 + 3 \\
\hline
3 \times 4 &= \quad 12 \\
3 \times 30 &= \quad 90 \\
20 \times 4 &= \quad 80 \\
20 \times 30 &= \quad 600 \\
\hline
&\quad 782
\end{aligned}
$$

Figure 5.10   A generic rectangular diagram can be labeled to serve as a graphic organizer for multiplying two-digit numbers.

DISCUSSION OF THE   ■
MATHEMATICS TEACHING EXAMPLE

In this teaching example, a variety of visual representations were used to help students think about the concept of multiplication with large numbers, and to illustrate connections to symbolic forms and algorithms for two-digit multiplication.

Mathematics Goals

Ms. Walker has a long-term goal of having her students understand the structure of multidigit multiplication—that is, multiplication that is based on partial products—and to use this knowledge to find products. She wants to expand her students' number sense and particularly their estimation skills. In the process of achieving these goals, students are supported as they use a variety of rectangular diagrams to display and discuss mathematical work.

The teacher carefully lays a foundation for making connections between students' work with models, the recording and labeling of students' visual work, the specific procedures used with multiplication algorithms, and the product. The teacher is aware that students often make errors such as the error shown in Figure 5.1 if they begin to use the standard algorithm for multiplication without understanding why there are actually four partial products for a problem such as 34 rows with 23 chairs in each row.

The students' initial experimentation with tallies, tiles, and other methods helps them grasp the magnitude of the product of a problem such as 23×34. By discussing the relative efficiency of each method, the students were led through guided discovery to see the value of using an array or area model to represent two-digit multiplication.

The students' use of base-ten materials and rectangles on grid paper builds a foundation for the important goal of recording the four parts to a product for two-digit multiplication.

The use of the rectangular diagrams, which initially represent arrays with rows and columns, will be an important foundation for understanding an area model in which the dimensions represent length and width and the product is a number of square units. The rectangular diagrams also are related to expanded notation and to the distributive property, for example, $23 \times 34 = (20 + 3)(30 + 4)$.

Language Goals

The teacher clearly embedded many connections between academic language and visual representations. Students had many opportunities to develop concepts and vocabulary through listening and speaking. There is also direct teaching of verbal forms for reading a number sentence, for example, $23 \times 34 = \_\_$ can mean "Twenty-three rows with thirty-four things in each row equals what number?"

Use of an Advance Organizer

The warm-up worksheet, prepared in advance by Ms. Walker, serves as an advance organizer by giving students practice with previously taught academic language vocabulary words that are essential to the lesson. The students are able to refer to the worksheet during discussions and when labeling their own array drawings. By focusing on Number 8 with the whole class, the teacher stresses an idea that is a foundation for understanding partial products: arrays can be subdivided into parts to simplify the process of finding a total. Also, breaking the factor 6 into two parts such as 5 and 1 is a foundation for thinking of a factor such as 23 in its expanded form of 20 plus 3.

Ms. Walker uses the warm-up time with the advance organizer sheet to listen to and monitor group conversations, assessing what the students know. At the same time, she moves the class along. She waits to check the students' completed papers after class.

The verbal connection that is made to prior learning through the discussion of the class's recent experience solving a problem by counting by fives also serves as an advance organizer. It helps the teacher make sure all students understand the context of the current problem and reminds them that this could be thought of as another repeated addition, or skip-counting problem, but a more efficient method should be discovered. Ms. Walker also helps students understand the current problem by having them visualize the size of the multipurpose room.

Visual Learning Strategies, Cognitive Tasks, and Language Development

Beginning with a story and picture, and having the students work in groups, provides students with access to the lesson. It also provides opportunities for students to practice their Basic Interpersonal Communication Skills (BICS), their use of everyday language. The teacher's instruction and facilitation are clearly geared to the cognitive domain where students are expected to develop important grade-level mathematical conceptual understanding and skills. In modeling academic language throughout the lesson through hands-on, visual, and discussion-based activities, the teacher bridges from BICS to the Cognitive Academic Language Proficiency Skills (CALPS) domain (Cummins, 2000). All of the instruction is organized with what Cummins calls cognitively demanding but context-embedded tasks. The teacher offers students access to context clues for learning by using a variety of visual methods such as drawings of rows and by scaffolding the use of base-ten blocks. The goal of instruction is clearly to move to greater levels of abstraction, but always with appropriate instructional support and understanding.

The teacher gave well-planned guidance that led to students being able to draw, label, and use their own drawings. First, she had them review prior experiences with problems involving rows of equal numbers. Next, they related the rows to labeled lines within a rectangle and made connections to both the base-ten block display made by a group of students and to rectangular arrays drawn on grid paper. Initial direct assistance was offered to the English learners as they drew on grid paper. The students' drawings, including array diagrams, allow the students to communicate by looking and gesturing, rather than relying solely on listening and talking. Drawings serve as a bridge between the understanding developed while working with the base-ten blocks and more abstract and cognitively demanding methods of using symbols to multiply. When posted, the drawings serve as visual reminders of new learning and vocabulary.

TEACHING TIPS ■

- Use physical models, acting, and Total Physical Response (TPR) to clarify the contexts of problems and to demonstrate relationships. For example, make equal groups of people to model a multiplication problem.
- Encourage students to visualize a problem situation, to imagine the action in the problem, and then to talk about it.
- Offer visual access to new concepts and vocabulary and reminders of prior learning by presenting and posting labeled illustrations and records of student work.

Figure 5.11 Records of students' ideas can be posted as visual reminders of discussions.

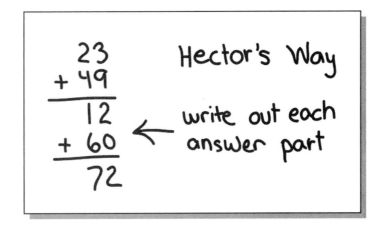

- Model and encourage student use of visual representations to help English learners see what other students are doing and to help students monitor their own understanding.
- Plan for specific instruction that helps English learners understand how to create their own graphic organizers and diagrams.
- Make posters or flashcards that show labeled arrays, and have students visualize arrays as they learn and use the multiplication table, for example, 6×8 as 6 rows of 8 dots and also as 5 rows of 8 and 1 more row of 8.
- Have students construct and label their own models and draw and label illustrations when learning about concepts such as perimeter, area, volume, and surface area.
- Use comparative organizers such as compare and contrast tables or Venn diagrams to help students build new understanding and integrate known ideas with new ideas or concepts.
- Work together as a class to develop diagrams that show addition with subtraction, and multiplication with division relationships.
- Ask students why specific posted graphic organizers, including charts, are useful and what they show or model.

Figure 5.12   Venn diagrams can be used for a variety of mathematical purposes.

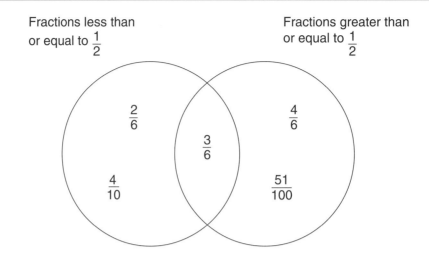

■ DISCUSSION OF VISUAL LEARNING IN MATHEMATICS

Students acquiring English often encounter mathematics instruction that is wordy, abstract, and defined by symbols. They are expected to read, comprehend, and remember information, directions, and expected outcomes as they struggle to learn the mathematics at hand in a language they have yet to acquire.

Visual tools make it possible for students to receive input that does not solely rely on the spoken or written word. While manipulative materials, demonstrations, and Total Physical Response give some visual information, specially structured visual forms give the added benefit of cuing the student during repeated encounters and can increase student-to-student communication.

What are graphic organizers, advance organizers, and diagrams, and why are they important?

Visual organizers provide English learners with visual images of content and academic language. They are used to organize important aspects of a concept or idea into an arrangement with identifying labels. They make it possible for the teacher to model or demonstrate expected processes and to monitor student understanding. In mathematics, these tools provide a frame or template for visually identifying essential facts and processing given information for the purpose of identifying relationships and solving problems.

Graphic organizers are visual structures that make it possible to organize words, ideas, information, and so on to further learning goals such as understanding, communicating, and remembering.

In mathematics class, graphic organizers are structures that assist students in identifying patterns and relationships. For example, a set of data may be organized by using a bar graph, tally table, line graph, and graph in the x-y plane. Also charts, concept maps (mind maps), and flow charts help organize and display similarities, differences, and connections between ideas. Number lines are forms of continuum scales that reveal many relationships among numbers.

One example of a graphic organizer is the two-column chart, sometimes informally called a "t-chart" or "t-table." (See Figure 3.2 on page 32.) It is an excellent tool for examining number patterns, engaging in logical reasoning, predicting values, and determining function rules. Another example is the Venn diagram opposite (Figure 5.12). Young children use Venn diagrams to sort and classify objects and as survey tools. Older students use them to explore sets and subsets.

Diagrams are a special type of graphic organizer that represents the structure of a mathematical problem but not surface features such as the context of the problem. They may be used to guide thinking, to make connections, and to help students attain concepts. The base-ten block figures were a transitional stage between showing a drawing of a representation of rows of chairs and being able to represent any two-digit multiplication problem with a diagram that shows areas for four partial products (Figures 5.5–5.10).

Diagrams can be used effectively to build conceptual understanding and to illuminate connections between operations such as addition and subtraction and among problems with similar mathematical structures. However, it is important to avoid teaching diagrams by rote; the purpose should be to assist with reasoning rather than to satisfy a requirement to produce a picture. For example, when learning to draw bar diagrams to represent addition and subtraction part-part-total situations, a class should repeatedly discuss the meaning of the various regions and labels of every diagram that is produced until the relationships become second nature (Figure 5.13).

Advance organizers are graphic organizers, that is, visual organizational frameworks of knowledge or information, that are planned ahead and that are often used to set the stage for a lesson. They may be used at the beginning and during the lesson to connect new ideas and abstract concepts to past learning or experience (Marzano et al., 2001; Newell, 1984). They help students become oriented toward the lesson content, retrieve what they already know about a topic, and be ready to focus on the new information (see Figure 5.2). Equally important, advance organizers are also used to promote active learning and communication during a lesson. For example, before a lesson, a teacher may prepare a poster with a two-column chart to

Figure 5.13   Bars are commonly used to represent "part-part-total" addition and subtraction relationships. Possible problems include: "How much must be added to 35 cents to equal 50 cents?" or "I started with 50 cents and spent some money, then had 35 cents left. How much did I spend?"

← 50 cents →	
35 cents	x

fill in with the class, or a number line to facilitate thinking about a specific problem (shown in Figure 5.14). In the lesson example in this chapter, the teacher began the lesson by having the students work on a warm-up with simple problems that they had previously solved. After briefly revisiting the essential vocabulary related to drawing arrays, she moved on to the lesson of the day.

Figure 5.14   Number lines are powerful mathematical visual representations. This diagram and problem may be used as an advance organizer.

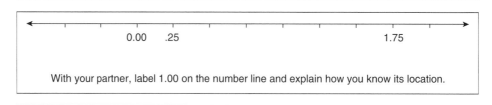

With your partner, label 1.00 on the number line and explain how you know its location.

Mathematics Visual Organizers

Visual organizers can help us do the following:

- Organize information
- Activate and develop prior knowledge or experience
- Focus on essential aspects of a lesson
- Record and arrange different bits of information so that mathematical relationships can be discussed and studied
- Serve as supporting information when justifying ideas or predictions
- Show connections between students' words and ideas and ways of organizing and illustrating their thoughts
- Provide a springboard for mathematical discussion
- Help students understand what processes or outcomes are expected of them
- Illustrate or document what students know or understand, especially if they lack fluency or writing skills to explain in words

Are all learners visual learners?

Some of us learn more easily by seeing, others more easily by hearing, and others more easily through physical experiences. Auditory instruction for students gives experience with a language's sound, cadence, and gestures and awareness of common sentence structures. However, until a student is at fluency Level 3, very little content can be learned solely through teacher talk or auditory instruction. English learners at early stages of proficiency *must* rely on visual input no matter what their preferred learning modalities.

The intent of a visual tool is not perfectly obvious to all viewers. In fact, different viewers may have different interpretations. Thus, careful teacher efforts are needed to build shared meaning each time a visual tool is used. The results should be increased content understanding and strengthening of each student's visual learning skills. Furthermore, there are some concepts, such as identifying patterns, universal symbols, or warning signals that rely upon a student's capacity to understand without depending on language (Levine, 2002). For example, in observing patterns, students may predict missing or extending elements by making visual sense of the existing pattern. They may manipulate shapes in their mind without needing language. They base their interpretation on their past experiences, including cultural and academic experiences. In the case of recognizing and extending a pattern, it is still helpful to know words that represent elements of the pattern.

Visualizing skills are also important when making sense of contextual problems. For example, making a mental picture of a word problem situation can serve as a springboard for identifying the underlying mathematical relationships.

VISUAL LEARNING RESEARCH   ■

Visual tools help students attain new concepts and see connections between language and content as they broaden understanding through a series of related activities. For English learners, visual learning strategies serve as support for understanding and communicating about ideas or processes. For example, diagrams, maps, charts, and tables can be used to organize new information, to reinforce what is being learned, and to cue memory at a later time. There is a correlation between increased activity in the brain and the explicit creation of nonlinguistic representations (Gerlic & Jausovic, 1999). Helping students discuss visual tools can enable students to understand more deeply, and to recall and retrieve information (Levine, 2002). According to the "dual-coding" theory (Paivio, 1990), knowledge is stored in two ways, nonlinguistic, or imagery, and linguistic. Imagery becomes critical for English learners as they transition into the target language. For example, all students benefit from imagining a polygon such as a regular hexagon, moving it around in their mind's eye, and seeing its attributes.

Being able to visualize a situation, to generate mental pictures (Willoughby, Desmarias, Wood, Sims, & Kalra, 1997) and draw a diagram are particularly advantageous visual learning and communication techniques (Guay & McDaniel, 1977; Hembree, 1992; Payne, 1990; Shigematsu & Sowder, 1994). Mendieta (2005) has devised a program for teaching students to use diagrams and other pictorial representations to represent concepts throughout the strands of mathematics. Smith (2003) points out that student-created representations offer valuable insight into a students' understanding and level of generalization. He also cautions that "multiple representations presented by different children may appear similar . . . [but], [c]hildren may view and use them in different ways" (p. 273). Graphic organizers used by students not only can facilitate learning, but also can serve as tools for evaluation and assessment by the teacher and for self-assessment as well as peer assessment (O'Malley & Valdez Pierce, 1996). Dominguez (2005) points out that English learners' gestures may also provide important information on students' mathematical reasoning and level of mathematical knowledge.

It is neither sufficient to post visual tools nor to simply model their use. Visual learning tools are specific cognitive learning strategies that enable the learner to mentally manipulate the material to be learned and that should be purposefully taught to English learners (Chamot & O'Malley, 1994). For example, graphic organizers are most effective when students have in-depth instruction in their use and when they construct their own (Dunston, 1992). The teacher must model the process for English learners so they can have a clear understanding of what is expected, the meaning of the representations, and appropriate times to use each visual tool. It is also important to use topics that are of interest to students as a context for instruction. For example, favorite television shows, music, or food are often used to teach students how to create graphs or analyze data.

Repetition of new concepts through various contexts, sometimes referred to as "concept redundancy," helps students to build robust, lasting understanding (Cohen, 1994). For example, students may be asked to match word problems with number sentences, diagrams, or other representations.

Sternberg and Spear-Swerling (1996), among others, emphasize that guided creative thinking activities can be helpful in promoting concept formation in mathematics and across the content areas. For example, a teacher might ask, "How can nine-twelfths ($\frac{9}{12}$) and seventy-five hundredths (0.75) refer to the same quantity? What do you think of when you see or hear these numbers? What do you see in your mind? What are ways to show this idea?"

■ PRACTICE AND DISCUSSION QUESTIONS

1. Describe what you currently do in your math class to help visual learners and make an annotated list of additional specific techniques that you will try.

2. Briefly describe an upcoming mathematics lesson topic. How would you design an advance organizer to support English learners' learning? How would it be of help?

3. In the teaching example, the teacher had the groups use different representations when they first explored the Problem of the Day. What do you think the teacher's purpose was? Was she addressing some of the teaching group's stated goals and stated student difficulties? Why did she not provide time for the students to finish the work the next day?

4. One teacher examined Figure 5.1 and commented, "Kids just 'carry' the ten and multiply in the tens and forget about the rest of the problem. They don't seem to know that 72 could never be the answer to a problem like 20 times 30—it has to be at least 600." Comment on Figure 5.1 and explain the error that students make. How would you incorporate visual learning strategies in your lessons to give students strong understanding and skill with such problems?

6

Questioning Strategies

*Ask Questions to Foster
Students' Learning of
Mathematics and English*

RATIONALE FROM RESEARCH ■

The teacher has an important role as the one who sets up situations that spark communication, who poses questions, and who models mathematical communication. Particularly for English learners, the questions that a teacher asks affect students' access to a lesson, the level of engagement, and the degree of mathematical learning that takes place. Questions can act as a catalyst for the use of spoken language.

The National Council of Teachers of Mathematics (NCTM) reminds us that "well-posed questions can simultaneously elicit, extend, and challenge students' thinking and at the same time give the teacher an opportunity to assess the students' understanding" (2000, p. 197). Unfortunately, studies indicate that teachers often ask questions related to what they perceive as interesting instead of what is critical to know about an idea or concept (Risner, Nicholson, & Webb, 1994). In addition, lower-level questions are frequently asked of all students, but even more frequently of English learners, based on their lack of English language skills (Gall, 1984). As part of a study involving extensive classroom observations across the United States, Weiss, Heck, and Shimkus (2004) commented that questioning "was among the weakest elements of mathematics instruction, with only 15 percent of lessons nationally incorporating questioning that seemed likely to move student understanding forward" (p. 29). Clearly, questioning is a powerful, yet underutilized strategy for supporting students' learning of mathematics.

Questions may be literal, for example:

"How far do you move on a turn?"

"What does the problem ask you to do?"

"What have you done so far to solve the problem?

Questions can also expand thinking or help students infer processes, for example:

"Why do you think that certain sums occur more often than some other sums when we roll two dice?"

"How might the results change if you used two ten-sided number dice to play the game?"

The following teaching example illustrates how questions from the lower comprehension and application levels to the higher levels of synthesis and evaluation can be posed to all students of varying language proficiency levels.

■ MATHEMATICS TEACHING EXAMPLE

Probability Introduction

Snail Races

A. Have a group of 3 or 4 players. You need a Snail Race Game Board, 2 dice with different colors, and markers.

Rules: Choose the snail that you think will finish first.

Take turns. Roll 2 dice. Add the numbers. Find the snail with that sum as its number. Put one marker on the snail's path to help it move forward one space.
   A snail is the winner if its path is full of markers first. Write down which snail wins after each game.

B. Think about playing this game on another day. Which snail do you think will win? Which will probably not win? Tell why.

Figure 6.1   Snail Race Game Board

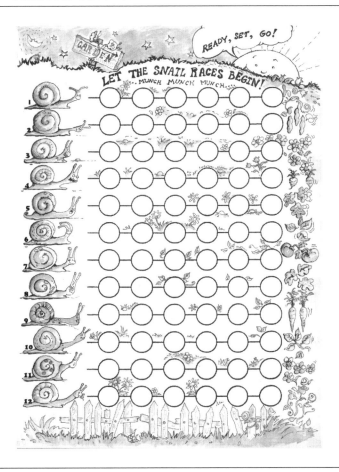

SOURCE: Coates and Thompson (2003). Reprinted from *Family Math II*, published by EQUALS, Lawrence Hall of Science, Berkeley, CA 94720. ©2003 Regents, University of California at Berkeley. For more information on *Family Math*, please see www.lawrencehallofscience.org/equals

In the following excerpts from a lesson, students in a Grade 3 class first play the game and gather data on winning snail numbers. (Instructions for the game and a full-sized game board appear as Exhibit A6.1 in the Appendix.) Then, the teacher asks questions of the whole class. The questions are annotated to indicate the type of question asked.

Excerpts From Lesson Dialogue	*Type of Question/Purpose*
T: Did you ever run in a race? Who has watched a race? What kind of race?	Connect to prior knowledge or experience

T: We have a game called Snail Race. Before we play, we will each guess, or predict, one snail to be the winner.
   On your turn you will roll two dice, like this. Then, you will add the numbers.
   You will help the snail with that number, your sum, move one space by putting one marker for it to sit on. Which snail will move on your turn? Who can tell about how the game works? Let's write some notes on the board.
	Monitor understanding
	Reinforce procedures

(Continued)

(Continued)	

Sts: I say which snail I think will win.
    We take turns.
    We add the numbers.
    That snail gets to move up.	

T: How far does a snail move on a turn?	Monitor understanding; direct recall
St: One. [Gesturing to one circle on the game board]	
The class reads the written rules together and compares the rules to their notes on the board. They then spend the rest of the math hour playing the game in groups of three or four. In order to begin to make a bar graph for the next day's discussion, the teacher gives each group a card for each game and asks that they write down which snail won. She walks around and asks questions that help make sure all the students understand how to play the game, and also asks questions that make some students begin to wonder whether it is a "fair" game. The next day, the teacher has the students play one more round and make a card for the winning snail before calling the class together for a discussion.	
T: Show on your fingers the number of the snail that you thought would be the winning snail. [The students show varying numbers.]	Monitor understanding and analysis of game
T: I noticed that no one chose Snail Number 1. Why didn't you predict, or choose, Snail Number 1? Tell your neighbor quickly, and then look up here.	Advance organizer Probing
[The teacher has prepared a large template for a bar graph and posts it at this time.] T: Help me label our bar graph. How can we use this chart to find out which snail won the most in our class?	Inference, logic Scaffolding chart-making
Sts: Write "Snail Game." Put all the snail numbers, 1, 2, 3, . . . and 12. Glue on the cards for the winners. Line them up by their numbers.	Building understanding Maintaining student engagement and participation
T: . . . Who has a card that says that Snail 2 won? [The students with cards for Snail 2 come up and they put each card on the graph. The same is done quickly for each possible sum.]	Visual cues Building and monitor understanding

Figure 6.2   Bar graph of Snail Race results, showing 18 trials.

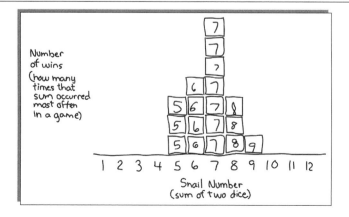

T: I also started a tally chart for us to use when we play today. How did I choose the numbers? How should we use this chart?	
St: They are snail numbers.	
St: Make a mark, a tally mark, if a snail wins.	
T: Let's do that. Look at our bar graph. Everyone, show me with your fingers how many tally marks we should put for Snail 1, for Snail 2. . . . to show about yesterday's games. [The teacher calls on students to draw the tallies.]	
T: Before you play the game again, think first, then talk to your neighbor about these questions on the board: Do you think that one snail will win the game? Which snail? Will it almost be a tie? Do you think many snails will almost win? After you talk, play one or two more games. After you play each game, take turns putting a mark on our tally chart. [The groups play for 20 minutes.]	Inference, logic, asking for student opinions
T: Look at our tally chart. There are 5 tally marks by Snail Number 5. Why are there 5 marks?	Monitor understanding

(Continued)

Figure 6.3   A tally chart of Snail Race results, showing the results after 24 trials (games).

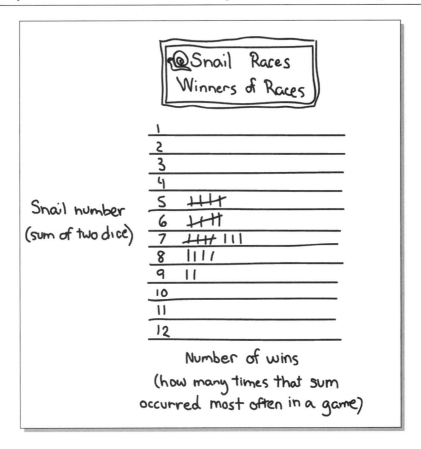

(Continued)	
St: It won 5 games.	
T: Good thinking! What fun, its number is 5 and it won 5 games. Do you think that Snail Number 11 should win 11 games?	Higher-level thinking, logic, and inference
Sts: No! It's hard to get 11. Yes, it's a high number. Yes, it's my lucky number.	
T: I heard someone say a new interesting idea, "It's hard to get 11." How can I get a sum of 11 on my turn? Imagine all the ways you can think of. What numbers do you see on the two dice?	Monitor understanding; scaffolded analysis
St: I see 6 and 5.	
T: What color was the die with the 6 in your imagination?	Scaffolding with visual cue
St: Red.	
T: Hmm. Interesting, I think you are imagining a 6 on a red die and a 5 on your white die. Who can say another way to get a sum of 11? [No response.]	Scaffolding
T: Think about your red die. Can it have a different number, not a 6, and still get a sum of 11?	Analysis Scaffolding
St: I get it!!! The red could be 5 and the white one could be 6.	
T: Now talk to your partner to see if there are other ways to get an 11. [They try starting with addends other than 6 or 5 and gradually realize that it won't work.]	
T: I heard two of you say, "If you get a 4 or any small number, you can't get to 11." Talk in your group about why you think this is true. [After two minutes, Sara is asked to speak to the whole class.]	Analysis
Sara: If you start with a 4, the other die can't help you get to 11. You need more than a 6.	Fostering student-student communication
T: What did Sara mean about "the other die can't help you get to 11"? Think by yourself, and then talk to your neighbor for a minute. Rigo, please say more about "the other die can't help you get to 11."	
Rigo: The highest number is 6 on our dice. You know, 4 plus 6 is only 10. Just 5 and 6 go together to make 11.	
T: Okay. It's time to think about our tally chart. When you are back with your group, take turns talking. Ask questions. Look at this poster of question starters for ideas of questions.	

Which sum happened _____ ? (most often; the least; *(number)* times)

Which snail will you pick the next time you play?

Please say more about why _____ .

What did *(name)* mean about _____ ?

During the ensuing 10 minutes of group discussion, the teacher listened in and wrote some quotes of student statements about the tally chart on a transparency. A whole-class discussion followed in which the statements were discussed and groups shared their observations.	Providing question and statement models to support speaking
T: Okay, now talk about why you think four different groups predict that Snail Number 7 is the best one to pick to win and why 7 was the biggest winner in our class. Write some notes on your group's recording paper. We'll then talk more about these ideas tomorrow.	Analysis; extending thinking Advance organizer

DISCUSSION OF THE   ■
MATHEMATICS TEACHING EXAMPLE

Mathematics Goals

The primary mathematics goal is to provide experience with a probability experiment in which the outcomes are not equally likely and to gather and discuss data. The teacher draws attention to the set of all possible outcomes by asking about Snail 1, which is an impossible outcome. By asking about Snail 5's and Snail 11's results, she also begins to distinguish between luck and favorite numbers and actual theoretical probability. The students also are introduced to the idea that a set of data is usually more reliable after many trials have been conducted and recorded.

Presumably, in future lessons, the class will investigate all of the possible addend pairs for each sum as a way of analyzing why certain snails win much more often than others. For example, an outcome of a sum of 4 only occurs three ways: with a roll of 2 then 2, or 1 then 3, or 3 then 1. But, a sum of 7 occurs six ways, with rolls of (1,6), (2,5), (3,4), (4,3), (5,2), (6,1).

The students also gain experience with the skills needed for constructing and interpreting bar graphs and tally charts and seeing connections between these two representations. Notice that the teacher asks the class for suggestions as to what labels to write and includes many students in the recording of data.

Also, the students have practice with basic addition facts as they take turns and check one another's moves.

Language Goals

There is an abundance of opportunities to speak and to listen to both the teacher and other students during the whole-class discussions and while playing the game. The posted questions offer English learners a structure for asking questions. The students listen to a description of the game, work as a class to write notes about the game, and also have a mini-lesson on reading the snail races game rules for the purpose of comparing the written rules to their notes on the board.

Multiple Goals When Asking Questions

The teacher asks questions of many levels of difficulty and for several different purposes, as is shown by the annotations in the lesson record. Some questions help students engage in higher-level thinking as they predict, analyze, and generalize. For example, several questions lead students toward the concept that the winning sums usually are those with many possible combinations.

The teacher's use of questions aims to include all students by making sure the game and the graph and chart are understood. For example, some questions focus on assisting with and assessing comprehension, or simply entice students to stay engaged in the lesson. Some of these are factual questions, such as, "Which snail will move on your turn?" or "Please explain" or "Please say more" requests.

The wide variety of questions is posed to all of the students, but students answer according to their level of fluency and according to their understanding of the mathematics concept.

Questions and Discussions Between Students

This carefully planned lesson maximizes students' opportunities to learn because it focuses on an engaging, challenging task. The activity provides constant opportunities for verbal interactions between students. Many interactions occur between students as they negotiate taking turns as they play the game, taking turns to record data, and as they converse during the game. Other interactions occur during the structured "Talk to your neighbor" moments. Having many chances to speak and to hear other students should benefit both mathematical and language development goals.

Notice that the teacher has purposefully focused on asking a wide range of questions rather than on telling the students what to do, how to do it, and what to think about the results of their experiments. The questions help students develop the important concepts and skills related to probability and data and also provide reasons to speak and to listen.

■ TEACHING TIPS

- Wait at least seven seconds after asking a question in order to allow students to think without needing to listen.
- Use students' answers as part of further probing questions (for example, "Why do you think a sum of seven happens so often?"), rather than rushing to say "Good" or "Thanks."
- Model question structures that students may use during class discussions; for example, "Why is ___ different from ___?" and "__(name)_, what did you mean when you said, ' . . .'?"

- Post a few question frames to use frequently during instruction for a period of several weeks in order to expand your repertoire.
- Begin some small-group discussions by posting a specific question for students to ask their classmates; for example, "Why do you think that . . . ?" or "Can you please explain to me . . . ?"
- Vary the level of complexity of questions for all students, but carefully decide which student to ask to respond verbally to each question depending upon their level of fluency and grasp of the mathematics topic.
- Ask knowledge and understanding (literal) questions that generally have specific, short expected responses and also ask questions that promote mathematical reasoning and higher-order critical and creative thinking.
- Direct some questions to particular students by name in order to show that you expect that they are thinking about the topic and to show your interest in their thoughts.
- Help students expand their responses by asking questions such as, "How did you think about it in your head?" "Tell us why you think . . ." and "Where did you start?"
- Avoid rushing through a lesson by letting the same few students answer most of the questions.

Figure 6.4   Question frames that are used regularly during discussions help extend students' thinking and create a familiar routine for all students.

> Who will say in their own words what *(name)* just told us?
>
> What other problem of ours is like this problem?
>
> Who will come to the board and tell us about another way to solve this problem?
>
> Which answer choices in this multiple-choice problem are definitely not correct?

DISCUSSION OF QUESTIONING ■ STRATEGIES IN MATHEMATICS

Communication, which includes asking and responding to questions, is a tool that promotes a thorough learning of mathematics.

The National Council of Teachers of Mathematics' Communication Process Standard (2000) emphasizes the importance of communication in the teaching and learning of mathematics:

Instructional programs . . . should enable all students to

- Organize and consolidate their mathematical thinking through communication
- Communicate their mathematical thinking coherently and clearly to peers, teachers, and others
- Analyze and evaluate the mathematical thinking and strategies of others
- Use the language of mathematics to express mathematical ideas precisely (*Principles and Standards of School Mathematics*; NCTM, 2000)

In addition, organizations such as the Center for Research on Education, Diversity and Excellence ([CREDE], 2002) have pointed out the value of dialogue over lectures:

> Thinking and the abilities to form, express, and exchange ideas are best taught through dialogue, through questioning and sharing ideas and knowledge.

Finally, many organizations, including TODOS: Mathematics for All, stress the importance of frequent opportunities to engage in meaningful communication about significant topics as a means of promoting both English language development and a high level of academic achievement.

How does placing a focus on questioning affect English learners and their teachers?

Placing an intensive focus on language during mathematics instruction has profound implications for teachers of English learners in terms of planning and in relation to reflection on teaching. One way to provide opportunities for listening, speaking, and writing in mathematics is by crafting well-planned questions. Asking questions that are meaningful and comprehensible to English learners requires that the teacher must know the level of fluency of the students as well as their prior experiences or knowledge of the topic being introduced. One must pose questions that challenge and engage students in ways that support the new learning and foster language acquisition. And it is essential to foster a supportive environment.

For an English learner, the cognitive process of actually answering a question by speaking becomes a complex, multilayered process. What is the teacher asking? What do the teacher's words mean? What does she expect to hear? What words should I use in my response? Can I respond in my language and have someone translate? What if I mispronounce the words? Will others make fun of me? Suddenly a question that the teacher perceives to be simple becomes an overwhelming request, and a student may fail to respond, or simply say, "I don't know."

It should also be noted that students from some cultural groups are reluctant to publicly ask questions, particularly of adults, and also may be hesitant to make conjectures. For students from cultures in which students are expected to wait to be asked before speaking, and where students are not expected to ask questions of elders, it is very important for the teacher to explicitly set the expectation for students to ask questions and express their opinions in the mathematics classroom. Otherwise, classroom discourse becomes an exercise in trying to participate in a game where only others know the unwritten rules.

When questions are posed as triggers for mathematical thinking and class discussion, an English learner with limited spoken language skills can be included through translations, native language discussions, and use of visual tools. Hand signals, diagrams, pictures, and number sentences are all possible nonverbal ways of conveying ideas.

Students learn to become critical thinkers about mathematics by carefully listening to, questioning, and considering the claims made by others. Students should have both small- and large-group opportunities to question and probe one another's thinking in order to clarify underdeveloped ideas. Moreover, since not all solution methods have wide-ranging merit, students must learn to critique the strengths and limitations of the methods and ideas shared by others.

Should the levels of questions we ask students change as their levels of fluency increase?

In the past, it was sometimes stated that the level of question asked of an English language learner should be matched with his or her level of fluency. But it is important to distinguish between thinking questions and verbal response questions. Obviously, students in early levels of English acquisition are limited in the complexity of the verbal responses that they are able to provide. However, this does not mean that in the mathematics classroom they should only encounter simple questions. Learning mathematics is a complex endeavor, requiring students to think about many ideas and their interrelationships. So, through the use of a mixture of strategies, higher-level thinking questions must be made comprehensible so that all learners hear questions such as, "How are fractions and decimals alike and different?" This question prompts thought about what is already understood and also comparisons that are likely to lead to a deeper understanding of both fractions and decimals.

Thinking questions (which certainly may also be verbally discussed) are often categorized:

- Direct recall
- Inference questions
- Probing questions
- Extending questions

Verbal response questions can be used to encourage students to consolidate their thoughts and speak aloud.

Questions that scaffold mathematical ideas are helpful to all learners. They focus student attention on an aspect of the concept, lead the student in a productive direction, help students compare and contrast ideas, and encourage students to decide what they think and what they wonder about. Question and sentence frames help provide guidance in formulating a verbal statement through scaffolding prompts and models of the expected language. Sample questions that support all learners are presented in Exhibit A6.2 in the Appendix.

How can we ensure that we are challenging our students through our questioning?

Questions that provoke lively conversation through the debate of a variety of ideas, that lead to attempts to explain and justify statements and solution methods, and that engage students in both teacher-student and student-student dialogue are likely to lead to growth for all learners. Such highly motivating questions encourage higher-level thinking and deeper, more connected mathematical understanding, and also provide an engaging context for developing the ability to speak about mathematics. Students with very limited ability to speak in English will have ample opportunities to listen to the ideas of others during discussion of challenging questions, and may still speak, or write, in their native language as a means of consolidating their understanding.

What are levels of questioning that can elicit verbal responses from students with various levels of English acquisition?

In the box below, we examine the types of questions that engage students and provide opportunities for verbal responses at the various levels of the cognitive domain and levels of proficiency in the target language. Notice that employing various levels of questions also provides all students, at various levels of mathematical understanding, an opportunity to speak. Also, it is important not to let language fluency levels limit exposure to questions because students' level of language fluency may not necessarily be related with their level of mathematical understanding.

Questioning Strategies and Language Proficiency Levels

Students in the beginning levels of learning a new language (students at Proficiency Level 1) can show comprehension by following directions, pointing, answering yes/no and agree/disagree questions, or through role playing. They can also label parts of drawings, illustrations, or graphs and diagrams.

Beginning Level (Level 1)

Level 1 questions for verbal response should be accompanied by physical or pictorial models and can include but are not limited to the following forms:

- Is this a circle? (yes/no)
- Is this a circle or a triangle? (either/or)
- Which is a circle? (identify shapes)
- Show me the blue circle. (shape and color)
- Point to the biggest circle. (size and shape)
- What is that? (single word response, "triangle")

Students in Level 1 can participate in mathematical investigations that require higher-level thinking and analysis, and they are capable of responding to more cognitively challenging questions in the language in which they think. In general, students at this level should be included in all classroom activities and not be isolated because of their English language level.

Early Intermediate, Level 2

Level 2 students are able to generate and speak simple sentences. Although they may make grammatical errors in speech, they reproduce familiar phrases, are acquiring grammatical elements, and can use content vocabulary to write sentences to express main ideas or points of a lesson. It is helpful to provide meaningful and familiar contexts for lessons as they move toward intermediate fluency. At this level, students can be asked to expand on who, what, and where (literal) questions.

They need mode of response models, sentence frames, and explicit instructions:

- What do we call this shape?
  This is a triangle. (simple sentence)
- Tell me about this shape.
    The triangles is red. (two characteristics with grammatical error)
    The triangle has three vertices. (may say "corners" if content vocabulary is not known)
    The triangle has straight edges or sides. (accurate description with restatement of one element)
    Triangles are good building because they are strong. (meaningful context, with extension)
    Students in Level 2 proficiency still need access to primary language (the language in which they think) to best explain their higher-level thinking skills of analysis, synthesis, evaluation, and conceptual understanding.

Intermediate, Level 3

Although the characteristics at this level of fluency are approximating early advanced fluency, it is important to note that most of the linguistic progress made to this point is social fluency. Students interact with native speakers and can be heard having social conversations with others without making the grammatical errors noted in Level 2. Academically, students can engage in conversations and produce connected ideas or narratives. Although they still require scaffolding, they can identify main ideas and details in the target language.

The following types of questions are appropriate at this level:

- Now that we have studied triangles, compare them to another polygon. (comparison)
    A triangle gots three corners. A rectangle gots four corners.
- Name three important characteristics of a polygon. (main ideas and extension)
    The sides go straight, it's flat, it doesn't have a door.
- Why do you believe that the triangle is a strong form for buildings? (evaluation, justification)
    It holds good. It don't fall down.
- Write four true things about your polygonal train. (open-ended, connecting narrative)
    My pattern is two trapezoids then one triangle. It is long. It has straight sides.

To ensure that all students have the opportunity to speak, the teacher may consider assigning paired dialogues or interviews. Other activities may include individual and group-directed problem-solving exercises, games, and opportunities to connect academic language to mathematics. At this level, it is also important to ask for verbal responses to how and why questions as well as other higher-level open-ended questions.

Early Advanced, Level 4

In the early stages of advanced fluency, students are continuing to develop academic vocabulary as well as content vocabulary. They are also moving toward

(Continued)

(Continued)

> grade-level literacy skills. Their social language, also referred to as Basic Interpersonal Communication Skills (BICS), appears to be well developed.
>
> Questioning strategies at this level may include the highest order of the cognitive domain, such as analysis of errors and perspectives, constructing arguments, and elaborating on an idea. Students may still require visual scaffolding and other accommodations for core content instruction and should be receiving formal grammar instruction in the target language.
>
> Students at this level should also be formulating their own questions based on modeling from the instructor and English Only (EO) students.

■ QUESTIONING IN MATHEMATICS RESEARCH

In school, students often are asked adult-generated questions that may begin with any of the following: *who, what, when, where,* and *how*. These questions are of a factual or literal nature. While they may be easier for an English learner to answer, they rarely engage the child in a lesson in meaningful ways. Questions that require more elaborate thinking and talking, such as "Why do you think that . . . ?" are rare during lessons. Weiss, Pasley, Smith, Banilower, and Heck (2003) found inadequate, low-level questioning in 66 percent of observed mathematics and science lessons. Also, according to research, students are usually not encouraged to *ask* many questions. Teachers ask about 27 questions for every pupil's one, and most are lower-level questions (Bromley, 1992).

Questions should be richer than "What answer did you find?" Questions can promote oral interaction among students and extend their academic talk. Deborah Short and Jana Echevarria, two researchers and developers of the SIOP (Sheltered Instruction Observation Protocol) model (Short & Echevarria, 2004), remind us that "teachers should talk less and engage students in extended discussions so that English learners give more than one-word responses" (p. 12). For example, a teacher might follow a student's initial comment with "Tell me more about that" or "Why do you think so?"

Questions can sometimes be used to gain students' attention, to activate prior knowledge, and to give a hint about what students are about to experience. For example, a question such as, "Have you ever spilled your soda when you poured too much into a glass?" can help students predict the focus or context of the upcoming lesson and also spark their curiosity. Students are more likely to learn if they connect new skills, such as estimating when adding or subtracting decimals, to what they already know about work with whole numbers and also to a situation involving mixing a glass of punch and overflowing the measuring container (Marzano, Norford, Paynter, Pickering, & Gaddy, 2001).

It is important for English learners of all levels to be presented with questions that promote various levels of thinking, including questions that they may not yet be able to answer orally (Chamot & O'Malley, 1994). For example, all students may be asked, "Which of these four problems was solved incorrectly? What is wrong with the solution?" But, not all will be able to reply with elaborate verbal explanations.

Mathematical tasks also often are stated in the form of questions. Henningsen and Stein (2002) point out that higher-level mathematics tasks have a positive effect on students' engagement in learning. "The tasks with which students engage provide the contexts in which students learn to think about subject matter. . . . [T]he nature of tasks can potentially influence and structure the way students think and can serve to limit or to broaden students' views of the subject matter with which they are engaged" (pp. 27–28). Higher-level questions and tasks require students to analyze information, to restructure information, or to apply what they know. Such activity leads to deeper thinking about the lesson and potentially leads to lasting learning (Marzano et al., 2001). Good questions also engage students in meaningful communication about significant topics, which is beneficial to language development.

PRACTICE AND DISCUSSION QUESTIONS ■

1. Think about the questions that you ask most often during mathematics instruction. (You may want to keep notes for several days.) How and why would you expand your repertoire of questions?

2. What types of questions should be asked of Proficiency Level 2 and Level 3 students during mathematics lessons? What should the teacher expect as a response, both verbally and by other means of communication? (You may want to select a particular mathematics concept as a context for your response.)

3. Discuss the meaning of this Teaching Tip: "Use students' answers as part of further probing questions, rather than rushing to say "Good" or "Thanks" and moving on." Give an example related to the probability lesson and discuss the underlying message that students receive when their answers are not evaluated, but become part of a longer conversation.

4. What are some strategies that you can use to support English learners in answering more cognitively demanding questions?

5. Reread the lesson dialogue. Pose further questions to assess student thinking or understanding of the Snail Race problem.

7

Comprehensible Input

*Combine Many Strategies to Develop
Mathematics Concepts Through
Clear and Effective Instruction*

RATIONALE FROM RESEARCH ■

Comprehensible input is more than a strategy; it is an overarching concept in the instruction of second language learners. The strategies and ideas presented in the previous chapters contribute toward comprehensible input or understandable delivery of ideas or information. This chapter reviews and pulls together purposeful development of conversational language and academic language, along with the use of scaffolding, concrete materials, visual learning, and questioning. The purpose of attending to comprehensible input is to make grade-level content, as well as the English language, accessible to English learners. Furthermore, it should lead to increased student ability to think, solve problems, and participate in discussions during mathematics class. Mora (1998) points out the importance of delivering carefully designed lessons that provide English learners with comprehensible input to maximize understanding and provide an academic challenge.

The term *comprehensible input* is frequently used to express the main goal of Specially Designed Academic Instruction in English (SDAIE) methodologies. Strategies advocated to provide understandable delivery of academic content include the use of manipulatives, the use of visuals, explaining vocabulary rather than just defining it, and allowing students to use their native language (Doty, Mercer, & Henningsen, 2005). Many general good teaching practices contribute to students' grasp of a lesson, such as relating to prior experience, using multiple modalities, and emphasizing opportunities to make connections to other known mathematics and among representations.

When discussing comprehensible input as a strategy, Echevarria, Vogt, and Short (2004) explain that it includes teaching while using slower speech and avoiding use of idioms, along with making sentence structure and vocabulary modifications according to students' levels of English proficiency. Another aspect is clear instructions for academic tasks. In addition, the use of techniques such as scaffolding, highlighting key vocabulary, and using familiar objects address the need to provide comprehensible input. Along with addressing multiple modalities through listening, speaking, reading, and writing (Herrell & Jordan, 2004), English learners benefit from physical (or kinesthetic) experiences and rich visual input (Echevarria et al., 2004; Mendieta, 2005).

The following teaching example illustrates how even a challenging, potentially confusing textbook problem can be used in a lesson with a class that includes students with a limited command of English.

■ MATHEMATICS TEACHING EXAMPLE

Perimeter and Multiplicative Scaling

Problem of the Day: Enlarging Rectangles

Draw a 4-cm-by-6-cm rectangle.

Find its perimeter.

Draw and label 2 different rectangles that have a perimeter that is 3 times as long as the perimeter of your 4 by 6 rectangle.

(You may use a ruler or dot or grid paper.)

Mr. Marcus's fifth-grade class has almost completed a textbook chapter on adding and subtracting fractions that includes applications problems involving perimeter. He is now presenting one of the challenge problems in the text to give additional practice with perimeter and to lead into a new concept. He has purposefully chosen this problem in order to introduce a new mathematical idea and related vocabulary: times as much and times as many.

Mr. Marcus begins the lesson with a quick, related review session.

Let's review, before we look at today's Problem of the Day. I am drawing a rectangle. Tell your neighbor how I am making it look like a rectangle.

Figure 7.1   Mr. Marcus drew a rectangle on the board for a quick review.

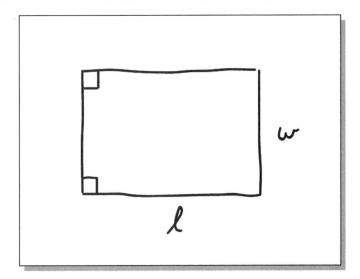

[Students give responses regarding square corners, straight sides, and four sides.] Everybody tell me, what do these letters, *l* and *w*, on my diagram mean? [All students respond "length" and "width" as the teacher touches each label and writes the words.] Tell your neighbor what we mean when we talk about the length and width of a rectangle. I'll take a quiet hand for someone who can share what you talked about. [Students offer "how long those sides are," "how many inches or meters long."] Remember, we used yarn to find the perimeter of our desks. Now, when I write the values for *l* and *w*, please think of the perimeter of the rectangle in your head. Watch, I am writing: *w* equals 5 cm and *l* equals 10 cm. Tell your neighbor the perimeter and how you figured it out. [As a review, a few students are asked to explain various ways of finding that the perimeter is 30 cm.]

Today we will work more with perimeter of rectangles, but we will be using this stretchy string [elastic thread] to think about perimeter. We will also use rubber bands and counters to help us learn what it means when we say "three times as long" or "five times as many" [pointing to phrases written on the board]. You will be working in your groups. Then, the whole class will discuss and solve our Problem of the Day.

Have you ever heard people say that they have ten times as many as someone else? [A few students share examples.]

Now, it is important to think more about these math words: "times as many" [pointing to the phrase on board].

Okay, take out five counters and put them in front of you, like this. [pause] You are showing me "one times as many as five," the same amount. Now put another row. [pause] Now put one more row. Everybody tell me, how many rows do we have? (Three.) How many are in the first row? (Five.) One way mathematicians describe what we are showing is to say "three times as many as five." [The teacher writes the phrase on the board as he is saying it.] Everybody say it: "three times as many." Tell your neighbor, what you have three times as many as. [pause] Who can share out what you said? [A student shares that there are five in one row and now with three rows that's three times as many as in just one row, so fifteen.]

Okay, clear your space and let's do that again. Now, show me one set—one row—of six counters. [pause] Now, show me three times as many counters. [pause] That's it, you have three sixes: six and six and six. We can write $3 \times 6 = 18$ to mean "three times as many as six counters is eighteen counters." Who already knew that? [No hands.] If I ask you to show me ten times as many as three, how many groups of three will you show? [Several students say ten.] What about fifty times as many as six, how many sixes? [More students say fifty.]

Figure 7.2   Notice that an array with three rows of six dots each also can be thought of as a representation for "three times as many as six counters is eighteen counters" and $3 \times 6 = 18$.

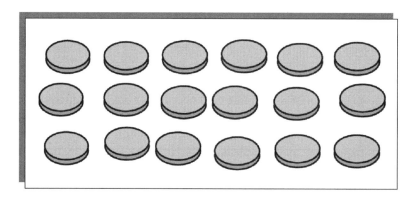

Now, clear away your counters. Start again with ten counters. Show me two times, or twice, as many counters. How many tens should you show? (Two.) [pause] How many counters altogether? (Twenty.) We can write $2 \times 10 = 20$ to mean "two times as many as ten counters is twenty counters."

Now, keep your twenty counters out. Who can show me half as many counters? [pause] Yes, when we find half of an amount we can split it into two equal groups and take one group. I can write $\frac{1}{2} \times 20 = 10$; let's read it together: "half as many as twenty is ten." What is half as many as ten? [A few students reply with "five."] We will keep practicing these ideas next week.

Now here's a fun and different way to think about "times as many"—and also "times as long." [Mr. Marcus points to the phrases in the problem statement.] Take one stretchy rubber band and a ruler

Figure 7.3   A rubber band is used to develop understanding of "two times, or twice, as long" by stretching it along a ruler.

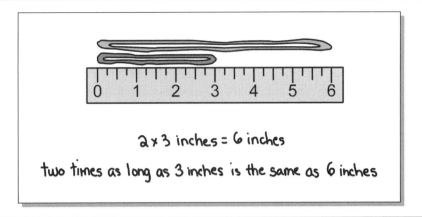

2×3 inches $= 6$ inches

two times as long as 3 inches is the same as 6 inches

from your basket. Hold the end like this [rubber band held down to 0 mark on the ruler]. Now stretch it to show three inches. How many inches long is it now? (3 inches.) Who can now stretch their rubber band so that it is two times, or twice, as long as before? [Writes "two times as long" on the board.] [pause] How many inches is two times as long as three inches? (6 inches) We can write 2×3 inches $= 6$ inches and read "two times as long as 3 inches is the same as 6 inches." We can use this stretching idea when we work on our Problem of the Day. [They practice a few more "times as long" rubber band problems.] Your group's materials manager should now collect and hold the rubber bands and rulers.

Now let's think about today's problem. It has clues, almost like in a riddle. [The teacher reads it aloud, underlining rectangle.]

First, draw a rectangle in the air. Yes, I see you are making four sides and square corners. What is the length; what is the width? [The teacher draws a rectangle on the board, roughly two-thirds as wide as it is long to correspond with labels of 4 cm and 6 cm.]

What is the perimeter of this rectangle? [Teacher underlines perimeter.] Tell your partner how you know the perimeter. [The students work in pairs, without difficulty, then discuss briefly with the class their reasons for stating that the perimeter is 20 cm.]

Okay, let's look again at the Problem of the Day statement and write a list of things to do. [Through questions from the teacher, various students contribute to the following list:]

1. Draw a 4-cm-by-6-cm rectangle.

2. Find the perimeter of your 4-cm-by-6-cm rectangle. (It is 20 cm.)

3. Figure how long is a perimeter that is three times as long as a 20 cm perimeter.

4. Draw and label two different rectangles that have the longer perimeter.

5. Remember to check your work.

Think about laying a stretchy rubber string around the perimeter of our four by six rectangle. How long should it be? (20 cm.) Look over here. This line on the board, and also my stretchy string, are 20 centimeters long, just like the perimeter around your rectangles. But, now the problem has a challenge. We are supposed to draw new rectangles that have a perimeter that is three times as long as our first rectangle. We must think about what we wrote for Step 3. When I read Step 3, I think, "How many centimeters long should the new perimeter be? We know the problem says it must be three times as long." Take two and a half minutes to think with your partner. How can we figure out how long the new perimeter should be? I will come around and collect your rubber bands and give your group a piece of stretchy string. [The teacher circulates and listens to students. First one pair, then others enjoy stretching their stretchy strings along a meter stick. Some later demonstrate that they counted by twenties, "20, 40, 60 cm" and, with the teacher's assistance, one student draws a line on the board that has a total of three 20-centimeter segments.]

So, are we finished? What does the Problem of the Day ask you to do? Yes, draw and label rectangles, with a perimeter of sixty. That's like a riddle for you to solve. [The teacher draws a somewhat larger rectangle, labeled "$p = 60$ cm," with arrows around the sides to remind students that perimeter is measured "around." He also demonstrates that either the stretchy string will need to be stretched to be three times as long, or the string will have to be used three times to go all the way around the new rectangle. Then, students work in pairs to draw two different rectangles with perimeters of 60 cm. They are left to grapple with this challenge in their groups of four. After a few minutes, Mr. Marcus decides a hint is needed.]

This problem might seem backward to you. We know the perimeter is 60 cm, but we have to figure out what the length, l, and width, w, equal. Hmm, what numbers will work? [He adds labels of "big l = ?" and "big w = ?" to his large rectangle.]

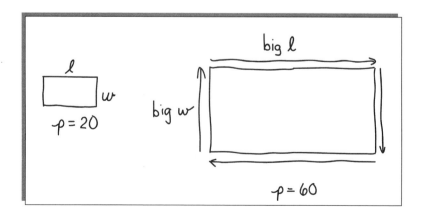

Each group proceeds to use a guess-and-check strategy to figure out values for length and width that will add up to 60 cm. Through informal discussion, they explore length and width values that do and do not add up to 60. They sketch and label several trial rectangles and record their work as addition, for example, as $10 + 20 + 10 + 20 = 60$. Mr. Marcus challenges one group to see if they can use fractions as side lengths.

Another group of students draws a rectangle similar to the one on the board and writes 10 cm and 6 cm as its labels. The teacher asks whether they have done "Step 5, check your work and make sure it makes sense." He then moves on to another group but continues to watch from a distance as a student realizes the perimeter is not 60 cm.

The teacher urges all groups to "practice saying why their rectangles are good answers to the Problem of the Day," in anticipation of a whole-class discussion. Each group prepares for the discussion by sending someone to draw and label a solution on the board. The groups are encouraged to also try to find a rectangle that no other group has found.

DISCUSSION OF THE ■
MATHEMATICS TEACHING EXAMPLE

As the lesson was planned and delivered, the teacher made many decisions that affected the degree to which the English learners, and all students, understood the lesson and developed the target concepts. Careful attention to delivery of comprehensible input is seen throughout the lesson. Strategies used include those discussed in earlier chapters of this book, along with creating comprehensible input by relating new learning to prior life experience, having a new experience together, using multiple modalities, and making connections to other known mathematics and among representations.

Mathematics Goals

Although the class has already studied perimeter, the teacher realizes that working with a problem where the perimeter is given, but not the length and width, would deepen students' understanding of the relationship among the three measures. The perimeter problem also serves as a context and launching point for discussing the important new concept of multiplicative scaling relationships represented by the phrases "times as long" and "times as many." Notice that the teacher begins with the basic concept of one times as many, the identity, and has students build a representation of three times as many as a lead-in to discussing the meaning of such phrases. The discussion includes connections among the spoken language, visual representations, and mathematical equations.

Because of the problem-solving nature of the Problem of the Day, the teacher has students work in small groups. As they invent and check many different solutions to the problem, the teacher does not specifically tell them how to proceed. The students have considerable arithmetic practice and encounter informal algebraic thinking. In a follow-up lesson, it is likely that the class would discuss how various solutions were alike and different and explore various related equations.

Language Goals

There is an obvious goal of developing and reinforcing academic vocabulary such as *times as many, rectangle, perimeter, length,* and *width.* Through repeated oral exposure, posting of words, reference to visual aids, and students' own experiments and drawings, these terms are reinforced. There is an additional language development goal related to having students listen to, and when possible give, explanations of their thinking and observations. The students are also assisted in reading with meaning the complex sentences in the Problem of the Day.

The lesson also is a foundation for thinking of mathematics as a language by making variables for length and width meaningful. It helps students develop diagrams and equations as a means of communicating complex ideas without being required to speak very much.

Teaching Decisions

Mr. Marcus decides to present one Problem of the Day as the context for reviewing past learning, for extending recent learning, and to introduce a new concept. If the lesson focused on worksheets with several different practice problems, a less coherent lesson would result, and some students might fall behind or complete work incorrectly without detection. Instead, this class makes continuous progress toward the teacher's mathematical goals.

Apparently the class has learned how to use tools such as rulers and rubber bands effectively and to work productively in small groups. The use of unusual concrete materials such as rubber bands and stretchy string (elastic thread from the fabric store) is likely to increase students' curiosity and engagement with the lesson and recall of the new ideas. The teacher structures part of the instruction around group work. The teacher decides not to model a correct solution to the problem but rather communicates his trust in each group's ability to find solutions.

Continuously Creating Access

Mr. Marcus incorporates a variety of strategies throughout the lesson and creates a safe, interesting learning environment. Prior to the main activity, the lesson focuses on a hands-on activity that serves to build and reinforce background understanding that becomes a foundation for concept development. Redundancy is built into the lesson; repeatedly in the lesson, essential terms and phrases are reviewed, used, and posted to keep them foremost in students' minds.

A friendly mention of "clues in a riddle" serves to lower anxiety about the complex written problem. Furthermore, the teacher guides the class as they work through the problem statement until it is comprehended. Then, he engages in a version of a think-aloud as he considers Step 3.

The phrase in the problem—"the perimeter is three times as long"—is presented as a curious mathematical clue to the students. It provides the teacher with an opportunity to introduce the class to the new concept, the meaning of multiplicative relationships of the "times as many" and "times as much" type. A foundation for understanding the new concept is built through use of models such as repeated groups of counters, string around a perimeter, and stretching rubber bands or stretchy string to find "three times as long."

Successfully Getting Started

Interestingly, the teacher does not begin the lesson by focusing on the Problem of the Day statement, nor by stating the goals for the day. Instead, recent, already understood concepts and procedures are reviewed and the first two steps of the problem are solved together as a class, without actually reading the complex problem statement. Presumably, this lesson order was chosen in order to create confidence in the students, to make links to prior learning, and to avoid creating anxiety about the day's goals. The main goals and expectations are stated just as the students are encountering the new ideas of "times as many" and "times as long." This makes it possible to relate the new concept to prior experiences and to teach it in a meaningful way as students are already engaged in the problem. The teacher also creates motivation, or an anticipatory set, by having the students stretch rubber bands.

Using Strategies to Provide Comprehensible Input

Mr. Marcus chose a challenging, potentially confusing problem as the focus of his lesson. By attending to issues of language and by using several instructional strategies, his class, including students with limited command of English, successfully completes the lesson.

Mr. Marcus paid close attention to *language* in his lesson. He reinforced vocabulary related to perimeter and purposefully built meaning for mathematical phrases and equations related to "times as many" and "times as long." He provided repeated exposure to key language.

Mr. Marcus *scaffolds learning* continuously during the lesson. He anticipated confusion with the problem statement and preteaches the important idea of three times as long. Then, rather than explaining the problem, he enlists the students' help in breaking the problem down into five necessary steps.

When the students reach the step at which they are to create new rectangles, Mr. Marcus does not model a correct response, because this is a problem-solving lesson. Instead, he has students work together in small groups and provides a diagram as a reminder or hint. He gives an additional "hint" after the first few minutes of group work.

Notice that the teacher recognizes the common error of finding factors that multiply to give 60 rather than finding a suitable length and width. He provides scaffolding by redirecting the students to their listed five steps rather than reteaching.

By using *concrete materials,* Mr. Marcus made the difficult ideas of the lesson comprehensible and fun for the students. Stretching elastic string to model three times as long turned potentially mysterious new academic language into something that not only can be modeled, but also imagined in the future. The initial uses of counters gave students an introduction to the new phrase in the context of a familiar representation. Notice, also, the teacher does not have students use squares, which usually measure area, nor cubes, which usually measure volume, to model the lengths of the sides of their rectangles, because he is informally drawing attention to the fact that length is one dimensional and because students often confuse area and perimeter.

Mr. Marcus incorporates *visual learning tools* into his lesson, in the form of labeled diagrams and posted vocabulary. The students also see several models of "times as many" relationships. Mr. Marcus also has students imagine, and draw in the air, rectangles with square corners, presumably as a way of cementing recent learning into long-term memory. Although the students would presumably already know about rectangles and perimeter, Mr. Marcus doesn't leave such important foundational knowledge to chance in this lesson.

Questioning strategies include asking questions at a variety of levels of complexity and inclusion of several thought-provoking questions. Some questions ensure that students understand basic information, such as how to find the perimeter of a figure; some encourage mental and physical active involvement in developing meaning for new concepts. Other instructions, such as to "practice saying why" not only give students an opportunity to speak mathematically, but also to self-assess what they do and do not understand about a problem, concept, or skill.

■ TEACHING TIPS

> Today we will learn about decimals and fractions that are exactly equal. We will find out why it is correct to say that 0.125 is exactly equal to $\frac{1}{8}$. Knowing this will be very helpful when solving many everyday problems, such as when shopping at sales.

- Provide a written clear purpose and reason for a lesson to help English learners become oriented to subsequent verbal and visual input.
- Refer to students' background knowledge and experiences and guide students to discuss prior knowledge and everyday situations that support a new concept.
- Tell students why a lesson is important and its connections to other known ideas.
- Begin teaching new concepts and skills through experiences set in a meaningful context in order to develop students' understanding and provide a common point of reference for the class.
- Tie new formal terms to students' experiences with the related concept and to their informal language used in discussions of the concept.
- Modify the language that you use by speaking slowly, using shorter sentences, and avoiding idioms and nonsense words.
- Consciously use body and facial gestures to enhance communication.
- Include purposeful redundancy and paraphrasing in explanations and discussions so that students hear a new idea several times.

- Give silent "think time" after all questions and before students interact with one another in order to allow all students to formulate their own mathematical thoughts and English learners to think about how to express their ideas in English.

- Involve students in frequent physical activities related to a lesson. For example, have several students measure a long length by sharing a single

ruler; and use objects, including students, to model mathematics problems.

- When the teacher writes brief notes of main points during a lesson, English learners see what new words are being pronounced and can see connections between words. Visual notes also serve as memory cues.

- Make lessons as visible as possible through use of posters, notes, graphic organizers, and equations on the board.

- As a class, develop and regularly use diagrams that represent key relationships involving the four operations.

- Use cooperative learning strategies to encourage students to build on one another's ideas, to assist others, and to receive help from classmates.

- Vary and integrate teaching strategies and materials to accommodate learning styles and to expand understanding.

- Seek ideas from colleagues, professional organizations, periodicals, books, and workshops.

DISCUSSION OF COMPREHENSIBLE ■
INPUT IN MATHEMATICS

The Five Standards for Effective Pedagogy,
Center for Research on Education, Diversity
& Excellence ([CREDE], 2004)

1. Teachers and Students Working Together to Create a Product or Idea

2. Developing Language and Literacy Skills Across all Curriculum

3. Connecting Lessons to Students' Lives

4. Engaging Students With Challenging Lessons

5. Emphasizing Dialogue Over Lectures

Planning a lesson with attention to comprehensible input is a challenging task. Yet, planning is essential if the *Five Standards for Effective Pedagogy* (CREDE, 2002) are to be addressed for English learners. When there are

English learners in a classroom, the teacher absolutely must go beyond using the spoken word and textbook to deliver instruction. The lesson plan should include basic strategies such as giving attention to prior experiences, highlighting visuals, using manipulatives, preplanning questions, and articulating goals. The lesson planning map in the Appendix is one resource that can serve as a reminder of diverse planning considerations. Additionally, a teacher must anticipate probable pitfalls, such as misunderstandings of words such as *three-quarters, change*, or *odd* and plan specific ways to monitor students' understanding.

How can we maximize students' comprehension of a mathematics lesson?

Garrison and Mora (1999) point out that using a new language to learn a new concept makes it quite difficult to reach both language and content goals. Ideally, a new, complex concept would be introduced in the primary language. Unfortunately, the reality is that many English learners are taught new concepts in a language that is relatively unknown to the students. Comprehension is likely to increase with the use of a variety of communication techniques, such as using simplified language, restating, using gestures, drawings, objects, and graphic organizers. *Simplified language* refers to the use of short sentences and avoidance of idioms, slang, and figures of speech. Before a teacher introduces formal English terms and gives elaborate explanations, it can be helpful to have students discuss and write about the new concept in their primary language. And, of course, efforts to use familiar contexts and known ideas create access and demonstrate cultural sensitivity. Teacher modeling, in the manner of a narrated "think-aloud," can also communicate expectations and meaning.

How is comprehensible input incorporated in the teaching of mathematics concepts?

Since conceptual understanding involves *understanding*, it is necessary for each student to work with a new concept in an actively engaged manner, thinking and talking all the while. Just as students work on their own to make sense of a reading passage, in mathematics they must think about what they understand and what they need to know and then develop and test new ideas. It is not effective to simply tell students what adults understand about a concept and expect them to immediately embrace the same understanding.

Comprehensible input strategies help English learners understand sufficiently to be able to tackle a new concept in a productive manner. Students' concept development can be supported by restating information in several ways, by asking questions that focus student attention on an aspect of the concept, by helping students compare and contrast ideas, and by encouraging students to say what they think and what they wonder about. Discussions, diagrams, pictures, demonstrations, and clear connections to other known concepts and to compelling real-world applications are also helpful.

What is the role of constant monitoring in English learners' mathematics classes?

Krashen (2002) speaks of an internal editor or "monitor" that self-corrects as we use language. In order for this monitor to work, a person needs to know the rules of grammar and have enough time for the correction to take place. The monitor can at times impede the flow of language because the speaker is too busy thinking of the rules to say what they want to say. Similarly, as students develop new mathematics concepts and skills, they should also learn how to monitor their work and understanding and self-correct as needed. For example, students should draw upon their number sense to solve problems, rather than checking an answer key or asking the teacher. Short periods of quiet, individual work time, sometimes called "think time," support both linguistic and mathematical self-monitoring.

When students are aware of their own level of understanding, the teacher can regularly monitor progress by using classroom signals such as thumbs up for "I agree," thumbs to the side for "I disagree," along with a wave over the head or across the chest for "I don't get it yet." Classroom signals give the teacher instant feedback and also keep students engaged. For example, a teacher might ask, "How well do you understand what 'three times as many' means?" or, "Thumbs up if your answer is less than twenty." It is also essential for the teacher to circulate and listen to small-group discussions and to look at student work during work periods in order to adjust instruction and continue to provide comprehensible input.

What is the role of thinking and learning strategies in English learners' mathematics classes?

In the Cognitive Academic Language Learning Approach (CALLA), students are explicitly taught learning strategies such as summarizing, cooperating, organizational planning, questioning for clarification, and using imagery (Chamot & O'Malley, 1994).

Thinking and learning strategies also include metacognitive strategies such as monitoring one's comprehension, making and then evaluating progress of plans for problem solving, and reflecting on one's overall learning progress. Cognitive strategies include ways of working with new information in order to develop new concepts and skills. In mathematics, examples of cognitive strategies include organizing and analyzing data, making visual or manipulative models of a problem, and identifying connections to prior knowledge. Social and affective strategies are also important learning strategies. Learning is facilitated when a student has the ability to work with others in ways that are comfortable to all. Social strategies include asking questions that elicit clarification of a statement and ways of working cooperatively toward a goal. Affective strategies include self-talk that increases or maintains one's self-confidence and reduces anxiety.

Learning strategies can increase learning by expanding students' ways of engaging with new content and new language (Chamot & O'Malley, 1994; Gersten & Jiménez, 1998; Herrell & Jordan, 2004; National Research Council, 2001). Students should be encouraged to think about what they understand, what they need to understand better, and what mathematics strategies work in certain situations.

■ COMPREHENSIBLE INPUT RESEARCH

Krashen (2002) has developed the Comprehensible Input Hypothesis as an effective approach for teaching a second language. It contains many elements that should be considered for teaching mathematics as well. In contrast to those who would advocate a grammar-based approach, Krashen contends that a student can learn a second language much faster if the input is understandable. Learners can relate to objects, pictures, and so on, thus increasing their grasp of challenging new words, phrases, and sentences. Krashen also emphasizes the importance of talking slowly and using speech that is modified to be helpful to the learner. Talking about an interesting topic that is related to "here and now," teaching from an understood point of reference, and providing plentiful context clues also contribute to language and potentially to mathematics concept acquisition.

Krashen is known for his "i + 1" teaching strategy. Students can extend their skills when the teacher takes comprehensible *input* and adds a *little* something new. The idea is to take students from where they are now, in a comfortable place, and to add something new. With proper support, students expand their learning. It is similar to the concept of teaching in the "zone of proximal development" (Khisty & Viego, 2005; Vygotsky, 1978).

Overshadowing all of the discussion about comprehensible input is the concept of an "affective filter." Krashen and Terrell (1983) hypothesize that comprehensible input does not impact learning directly, but passes through the learner's emotional state, which influences the quality of language learning. This affective filter includes three variables: the learners' degree of self-confidence, amount of motivation, and the level of anxiety. When the affective filter is low, students are confident, motivated, and comfortable in their classrooms and not nervous about making errors. When teachers work to keep the affective filter low, students are better able to learn; that is, the comprehensible input gets through (Dale & Cuevas, 1995). It is probable that a similar affective filter comes into play in relation to learning mathematics. Designing mathematics instruction with English learners in mind includes a systematic treatment of comprehensible input strategies, combined with maintaining students' self-confidence, high motivation, and capacity for risk taking.

■ PRACTICE AND DISCUSSION QUESTIONS

1. Think about teaching a small group of intermediate-level English learners the concept of perimeter. What would you say and how would you create access in your explanation? What would the students see? How would you assess students' learning?

2. What mathematical ideas did the students in Mr. Marcus's class work with? Give examples. What did Mr. Marcus do to make each idea comprehensible? How would you proceed with the next lesson for students in Mr. Marcus's class?

3. Use three or more strategies to show how you might make the following division problem accessible to students: 28 ÷ 6.

4. Why do you think classroom climate, and more generally, the affective domain, have a large impact on student engagement and learning? What goals will you have for your classroom in order to maximize students' comprehension and learning?

Appendix

Exhibit A1.1

Geometric Shapes

Shapes to copy and cut out for sorting activities. See Chapter 1 Teaching Example.

Exhibit A3.1

Blank Planning Map for Effective EL[1] Mathematics Lessons

This map is intended to illustrate the complexity of thoughtful, intentional planning that can go into mathematics lesson preparation for English learners. It is designed to help teachers engage in reflective lesson preparation for English learners and expand their practice by selecting from these strategies, and collaboratively planning, observing, and discussing mathematics lessons for English learners with colleagues. It is not intended as a lesson template.

LESSON SPECIFICS	LANGUAGE PLANNING AND GOALS	
Math Topic and Objective	ELD[2] Objectives and Standard(s) (including speaking, listening, reading, and/or writing goals)	Vocabulary to Reinforce
Standards	New Vocabulary that Needs Scaffolding and Possible Techniques to Use (plans for exposure, sense-making, practice, repetition, reinforcement, and application. E.g., ideas on how to demonstrate, explain, and post key vocabulary; help students create posters; make chart of lesson notes that include key vocabulary)	
Lesson Source or Textbook Pages		
	LEARNING SUPPORT PLANS	
Specific Problem Numbers and Main Purpose of each	STRATEGIES FOR SUPPORTING ELD Fluency Level 1 AND 2 ENGLISH LEARNERS (primary language support, realia, etc.)	STRATEGIES FOR SUPPORTING L3 AND L4 ENGLISH SPEAKERS (written language models, charts, etc.)
Sample Goal Problem	QUESTIONS TO FURTHER ELD GOALS	PLAN FOR GROUPING STUDENTS (individual; pairs; cooperative groups; whole class)

[1] EL is often used to refer to English learners, as ELL, ELD, and LEP have been used in the past.

[2] ELD is used to stand for English language development.

(Continued)

Exhibit A3.1 (Continued)

LESSON DELIVERY STRATEGIES		
REVIEW OF RELATED PAST LEARNING: WHAT and HOW (quick practice with foundational ideas, possibly in standardized test format)	IDEAS FOR LAUNCHING THE LESSON (connect to culture, prior experience, related math ideas. Engaging, motivating short verbal anecdote or demo or exploration in Warm-Up or Lesson Focus Problem.)	ACTIVE LEARNING EXPERIENCE (manipulatives, drawing, acting out, etc.)
VISUAL INPUT (modeling, graphic organizers, diagrams, etc.)	GUIDED PRACTICE PLAN (scaffolding plans)	QUESTIONS TO FURTHER MATH GOALS (to draw out possible misconceptions, highlight connections, help students deepen and generalize understanding)
	PLAN FOR SENSE MAKING AND PRACTICE IN STUDENT GROUPS	
FORMATIVE AND/OR SUMMATIVE ASSESSMENT PLAN (check for understanding)	MAIN ANTICIPATED POINTS TO ELICIT FROM STUDENTS DURING CLOSURE	STUDENT REFLECTION (writing prompt, Think-Pair-Share, etc.)

Exhibit A3.2

Lesson Planning Map: Example From Chapter 3—
Planning Map for Effective EL[1] Mathematics Lessons

This map is intended to illustrate the complexity of thoughtful, intentional planning that can go into mathematics lesson preparation for English learners. It is designed to help teachers engage in reflective lesson preparation for English learners and expand their practice by selecting from these strategies, and collaboratively planning, observing, and discussing mathematics lessons for English learners with colleagues. It is not intended as a lesson template.

LESSON SPECIFICS	LANGUAGE PLANNING AND GOALS	
Math Topic and Objective *Algebraic thinking: patterns in linear functions; modeling for problem solving; representations*	ELD[2] Objectives and Standard(s) (including speaking, listening, reading, and/or writing goals) *Listening to spoken models* *Use spoken models to explain thinking and to demonstrate understanding. (I noticed that . . .)* *Say 3 statements as part of a small group*	Vocabulary to Reinforce *arrange* *separate* *methods* *row* *fewer* *how many more* *variable* *mathematics rule* *mathematics expression*
Standards *Intro to: Alg 1.1, 1.4*		
Lesson Source or Textbook Pages *NA*	New Vocabulary that Needs Scaffolding and Possible Techniques to Use (plans for exposure, sense making, practice, repetition, reinforcement, and application. E.g., ideas on how to demonstrate, explain, and post key vocabulary; help students create posters; make chart of lesson notes that include key vocabulary) *2-column chart for each;* *for every label*	
	LEARNING SUPPORT PLANS	
Specific Problem Numbers and Main Purpose of each *NA*	STRATEGIES FOR SUPPORTING ELD Fluency Level 1 AND 2 ENGLISH LEARNERS (primary language support, realia, etc.) *Arrange for seating with language buddies*	STRATEGIES FOR SUPPORTING L3 AND L4 ENGLISH SPEAKERS (written language models, charts, etc.) *written prompt for small groups—look at 2-column chart, think, and discuss patterns; then say and maybe write 3 true things*
Sample Goal Problem *Number of seats with 10 tables*	QUESTIONS TO FURTHER ELD GOALS *What did you notice?* *How many more seats?*	PLAN FOR GROUPING STUDENTS (individual; pairs; cooperative groups; whole class) *Whole class and small group*

[1] EL is often used to refer to English learners, as ELL, ELD, and LEP have been used in the past.

[2] ELD is used to stand for English language development.

(Continued)

LESSON DELIVERY STRATEGIES

REVIEW OF RELATED PAST LEARNING: WHAT and HOW (quick practice with foundational ideas, possibly in standardized test format) *Warm-up prompts—standardized test items involving additive patterns and also multiplication.*	**IDEAS FOR LAUNCHING THE LESSON (connect to culture, prior experience, related math ideas. Engaging, motivating short verbal anecdote or demo or exploration in Warm-Up or Lesson Focus Problem.)** *Connect to prior experience planning a party; tell story about arranging tables—Antonio and Maria's dilemma.* *TPR – move tables, "sit" and count people*	**ACTIVE LEARNING EXPERIENCE (manipulatives, drawing, acting out, etc.)** *TPR with pretend tables; work with square tiles, grid paper, and diagrams; making 2-column charts.*
VISUAL INPUT (modeling, graphic organizers, diagrams, etc.) *Gesturing and demonstrating during story about the situation. Students asked to imagine the situation, specifically the rows of chairs.* *Teacher and students model with materials; make diagrams on grid-paper; create and post t-tables; chart main vocabulary.*	**GUIDED PRACTICE PLAN (scaffolding plans)** *Scaffolded group work: starting a 2-column chart for both plans (emphasize meaning of columns and entries).* *Writing a rule for any number of tables arranged Antonio's way (e.g. $s = 4t$; s = # seats; t = # tables)* **PLAN FOR SENSE MAKING AND PRACTICE IN STUDENT GROUPS** *Develop 2-column chart; and see ELD Strategies below*	**QUESTIONS TO FURTHER MATH GOALS (to draw out possible misconceptions, highlight connections, help students deepen and generalize understanding)** *Why are there fewer places to sit when the tables touch?* *When you add a table to a long row, how many more seats do you gain?* *(name) says this pattern increases by twos. Who can explain why this pattern works for Maria's table plan?*
FORMATIVE AND/OR SUMMATIVE ASSESSMENT PLAN (check for understanding) *Show me with your fingers how many can sit if . . .* *Individual work on: How many people could sit at 10 tables pushed together? How do you know?* **What about 100 tables? How many seats? Tell how you would figure it out.*	**MAIN ANTICIPATED POINTS TO ELICIT FROM STUDENTS DURING CLOSURE** *When tables touch, there are fewer seats.* *A diagram helps us discuss rules, e.g. if you put 1 more table in a row, it has 2 more seats.*	**STUDENT REFLECTION (writing prompt, Think-Pair-Share, etc.)** *Tell your neighbor about one thing that you learned during this lesson. Be sure you use some math words.*

Exhibit A6.1

Instructions for Snail Races Game

Snail Races

This is about
playing with probability as we develop number sense.

MATERIALS
crayons
game board, page 23
40 beans or markers (small enough to fit in the game board circles)
two dice

REAL-WORLD CONNECTION
Sometimes we can predict events based on past experiences. For example, if it rained in your town every first week of December for the last thirty years, one might say it is almost certain that it will rain at the same time this year. We explore probability based on the outcomes of rolling two dice. This means that regardless of past experience, one cannot predict which two dice will come up next.

How

- One to four people can play this game. Use the game board on the next page. Each player must choose a snail they think will reach the garden first. Identify the snail as yours by coloring it or by placing your initials on it.

- In this game, you will find yourself advancing any of the snails including your opponents' snails.

- The first player rolls two dice and adds the numbers together. Place a marker on the first circle of the snail with that number.

- Keep taking turns rolling the dice. To advance a snail, place another marker on the next circle each time that snail's number comes up. This means that every circle in a snail's path is covered as it advances.

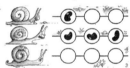

- Remember all the snails are racing. That is to say, you may have to place markers on a snail that is not your own.

- Keep rolling the dice until one snail crosses the finish line and reaches the garden for a tasty snack.

- Play at least four times. Keep track of the races you played and the snails that won.

- Which snails moved at a snail's pace?

- Which snails won the most? Why do you think this happened? Discuss any patterns that you and your family observed.

Game Board for Snail Races

SOURCE: Coates and Thompson (2003). Reprinted from *Family Math II*, published by EQUALS, Lawrence Hall of Science, Berkeley, CA 94720. ©2003 Regents, University of California at Berkeley. For more information on *Family Math*, please see www.lawrencehallofscience.org/equals

Exhibit A6.2

*Sample Questions to Support All Learners
and Develop Mathematical Thinking*

To help students rely on their own understanding, ask the following:

- Do you think that is true? Why?
- Does that make sense to you?
- How did you get your answer?
- Can you make a model or draw a picture to show that?
- What do you need to decide?
- Do you agree with the explanation?

To promote problem solving, ask the following:

- What do you need to find out?
- What information do you have?
- Will a diagram or number line help?
- What strategies could you use?
- Will you do it mentally? Use pencil and paper? Use a calculator?
- What tools or materials could you use to solve the problem?
- What do you think the answer will be?

To help students learn to reason mathematically, ask the following:

- Is that true for all cases? Explain.
- Can you think of an example that does not work (a counterexample)?
- How would you prove that?

To encourage conjecturing, ask the following:

- What do you predict?
- What would happen if . . . ? What if not?
- What might the pattern be?

To help students collectively make sense of mathematics, ask the following:

- What did you think about what _____ said?
- Do you agree? Why or why not?
- Does anyone have the same answer but a different way to explain it?
- Do you understand what _____ is saying?
- Can you convince the rest of us that your answer makes sense?
- What does your group notice about . . . ?
- What question could you ask the class about this problem?

To check student progress, ask the following:

- What have you found out so far?
- What else is there to do?
- What do you notice about _____?
- Why did you decide to organize your work like that?
- Have you thought of another way to solve this problem?

To help when students get stuck, ask the following:

- How would you say the problem in your own words?
- Would it help to draw a picture, make a model, or act it out?
- What have you done so far?
- What do you need to figure out next?
- Could you try it with simpler numbers or fewer numbers?
- Would it help to create a table, a graph, a number line, or other diagram?
- Have you compared your work with anyone else?
- What did other members of your group try?
- Tell me what you did the other day on the problem about _____. Is it similar?

To make connections among ideas and applications, ask the following:

- What other problems or mathematical ideas does this remind you of?
- How does this relate to _____?
- What ideas that we have already learned were useful in solving this problem?
- Can you give me an example of _____?
- Can you think of a general rule that works for all of these cases?
- Can you write a formula?

To encourage reflection, ask the following:

- Does your answer seem reasonable? Why or why not?
- Describe your method to us. Can you explain why it works?
- What if you had started with _____ rather than _____?
- What have you learned or found out today?
- Will this method work for all numbers?
- What are three things to remember from today's lesson?

SOURCE: Adapted from *Developing Mathematical Thinking With Effective Questions* by PBS TeacherLine (2002).

References

Barnett-Clarke, C., & Ramirez, A. (2004). Language pitfalls and pathways to mathematics. In R. Rubenstein & G. Bright (Eds.), *Perspectives on the teaching of mathematics: Sixty-sixth yearbook* (pp. 56–66). Reston, VA: National Council of Teachers of Mathematics.

Behr, M. J., Lesh, R., Post, T. R., & Silver, E. A. (1983). Rational-number concepts. In R. A. Lesh & M. Landau (Eds.), *Acquisition of mathematics concepts and processes* (pp. 91–126). New York: Academic Press.

Bickmore-Brand, J. (1990). *Language in mathematics*. Portsmouth, NH: Heinemann.

Bielenberg, B., & Wong Fillmore, L. (2005, January). Educating language learners—The English they need for the test—How can we help language learners overcome the disadvantages they can experience when taking high-stakes tests? *Educational Leadership,* 45–49.

Boaler, J. (2006). How a detracked mathematics approach promoted respect, responsibility, and high achievement. *Theory Into Practice, 45*(1), 40–46.

Brenner, M. E. (1994). A communication framework for mathematics: Exemplary instruction for culturally and linguistically diverse students. In B. McLeod (Ed.), *Language and learning: Educating linguistically diverse students* (pp. 233–267). Albany: State University of New York Press.

Bromley, K. D. (1992). *Language arts: Exploring connections* (2nd ed.). Des Moines, IA: Allyn & Bacon.

Bustamante, M. L., & Travis, B. (2005). Teachers' and students' attitudes toward the use of manipulatives in two predominantly Latino school districts. In L. Ortiz-Franco, N. G. Hernandez, & Y. De La Cruz (Eds.), *Changing the faces of mathematics: Perspectives on Latinos* (pp. 81–84). Reston, VA: National Council of Teachers of Mathematics.

Center for Research on Education, Diversity and Excellence. (2002). *The five standards for effective pedagogy.* Retrieved November 15, 2006, from http://crede .berkeley.edu/standards/standards.html

Chamot, A. U., & O'Malley, J. M. (1994). *The CALLA handbook: Implementing the cognitive academic language learning approach.* New York: Addison-Wesley.

Clements, D. (1999). "Concrete" manipulatives, concrete ideas [Electronic version]. *Contemporary Issues in Early Childhood, 1*(1), 45–60. Retrieved November 15, 2006, from http://www.gse.buffalo.edu/org/buildingblocks/News Letters/Concrete_Yelland.htm

Clements, D. H., & McMillen, S. (1996). Rethinking "concrete" manipulatives. *Teaching Children Mathematics, 2*(5), 270–279.

Coates, G. D., & Thompson, V. F. (2003). *Family math II: Achieving success in mathematics.* Berkeley, CA: Equals.

Cohen, E. G. (1994). *Designing groupwork: Strategies for the heterogeneous classroom* (2nd ed.). New York: Teachers College Press.

Cohen, E. G., & Lotan, R. A. (1997). *Working for equity in heterogeneous classrooms.* New York: Teachers College Press.

Cummins, J. (1984). *Bilingualism and special education: Issues in assessment and pedagogy.* San Diego: College-Hill Press.

Cummins, J. (2000). *Putting language proficiency in its place: Responding to critiques of the conversational/academic language distinction.* Retrieved November 15, 2006, from http://www.iteachilearn.com/cummins/converacademlangdisti.html

Dale, T., & Cuevas, G. (1987). Integrating language and mathematics learning. In J. Crandall (Ed.), *ESL through content area instruction: Mathematics, science, and social studies* (pp. 9–54). Englewood Cliffs, NJ: Prentice Hall.

Dominguez, H. (2005, Summer). Bilingual students' articulation and gesticulation of mathematical knowledge during problem solving. *Bilingual Research Journal*, 269–293.

Doty, R. G., Mercer, S., & Henningsen, M. A. (2005). Taking on the challenge of mathematics for all. In L. Ortiz-Franco, N. G. Hernandez, & Y. De la Cruz (Eds.), *Changing the faces of mathematics: Perspectives on Latinos* (pp. 99–112). Reston, VA: National Council of Teachers of Mathematics.

Dunston, P. J. (1992). A critique of graphic organizer research. *Reading, Research and Instruction, 31*(2), 57–65.

Echevarria, J., Vogt, M., & Short, D. (2004). *Making content comprehensible for English learners: The SIOP model.* Boston: Pearson Education.

Gall, M. (1984, November). Synthesis of research on teacher's questioning. *Educational Leadership*, 40–47.

Garrison, L., & Mora, J. K. (2005). Adapting mathematics instruction for English-language learners: The language-concept connection. In L. Ortiz-Franco, N. G. Hernandez, & Y. De la Cruz (Eds.), *Changing the faces of mathematics: Perspectives on Latinos* (pp. 35–48). Reston, VA: National Council of Teachers of Mathematics.

Genesee, F., Lindholm-Leary, K., Saunders, W., & Christian, D. (2005). English language learners in U.S. schools: An overview of research findings. *Journal of Education for Students Placed at Risk, 10*(4), 363–385.

Gerlic, I., & Jausovec, N. (1999). Multimedia: Differences in cognitive processes observed with EEG. *Educational Technology Research and Development, 47*(3), 5–14.

Gersten, R., & Baker, S. (2001). *Topical summary: Practices for English–language learners.* Eugene, OR: National Institute for Urban School Improvement.

Gersten, R., & Jiménez, R. (1998). *Promoting learning for culturally and linguistically diverse students.* Belmont, CA: Wadsworth.

Gibbons, P. (1993). *Learning to learn in a second language.* Portsmouth, NH: Heinemann.

Goldenberg, C. (1991). *Instructional conversations and their classroom application (Educational Practice Report 2).* Santa Cruz, CA: National Center for Research on Cultural Diversity and Second Language Learning.

Green, R. L. (2005). *Expectations: How teacher expectations can increase student achievement and assist in closing the achievement gap.* Columbus, OH: SRA/McGraw-Hill.

Guay, R. B., & McDaniel, E. (1977, May). The relationship between mathematics achievement and spatial ability among elementary school children. *Journal for Research in Mathematics Education*, 211–215.

Hembree, R. (1992). Experiments and relational studies in problem solving: A meta-analysis. *Journal for Research in Mathematics Education, 23*(3), 242–273.

Henningsen, M., & Stein, M. K. (2002). Supporting students' high-level thinking, reasoning, and communication in mathematics. In J. Sowder & B. Schappelle (Eds.), *Lessons learned from research* (pp. 27–35). Reston, VA: National Council of Teachers of Mathematics.

Herrell, A. L., & Jordan, M. (2004). *Fifty strategies for teaching English language learners.* Upper Saddle River, NJ: Merrill.

Idol, L., Jones, B. F., & Mayer, R. E. (1991). Classroom instruction: The teaching of thinking. In L. Idol & B. F. Jones (Eds.), *Educational values and cognitive instruction: Implications for reform* (pp. 65–119). Hillsdale, NJ: Erlbaum.

Johnson, D. W., & Johnson, R. T. (1990). Using cooperative learning in math. In N. Davidson (Ed.), *Cooperative learning in mathematics: A handbook for teachers* (pp. 103–125). Reading, MA: Addison-Wesley.

Kagan, S., Kagan, L., & Kagan, M. (2000). *Reaching standards through cooperative learning: Providing for all learners in general education classrooms: English language arts teacher's guide.* Port Chester, NY: National Professional Resources.

Khisty, L. L. (1995). Making inequality: Issues of language and meanings in mathematics teaching with Hispanic students. In W. Secada, E. Fennema, & L. Adajian (Eds.), *New directions for equity in mathematics education* (pp. 279–297). New York: Cambridge University Press.

Khisty, L. L., & Morales, H. Jr. (2004). *Discourse matters: Equity, access, and Latinos' learning mathematics.* Retrieved November 15, 2006, from http://www.icme-organisers.dk/tsg25/subgroups/khisty.doc

Khisty, L. L., & Viego, G. (2005). Challenging conventional wisdom: A case study. In L. Ortiz-Franco, N. G. Hernandez, & Y. De la Cruz (Eds.), *Changing the faces of mathematics: Perspectives on Latinos* (pp. 71–80). Reston, VA: National Council of Teachers of Mathematics.

Krashen, S. D. (2002). *Second language acquisition and second language learning* [1st Internet ed.]. Retrieved November 15, 2006, from http://www.sdkrashen.com/SL_Acquisition_and_Learning/index.html

Krashen, S. D., & Terrell, T. D. (1983). *The natural approach: Language acquisition in the classroom.* Englewood Cliffs, NJ: Prentice Hall.

Leinhardt, G. (1988). Expertise in instructional lessons: An example from fractions. In D. A. Grouws & T. J. Cooney (Eds.), *Perspectives on research on effective mathematics teaching* (Vol. 1 in a series of monographs from conferences of the National Council of Teachers of Mathematics, pp. 47–66). Hillsdale, NJ: Erlbaum.

Levine, M. D. (2002). *A mind at a time.* New York: Simon & Schuster.

Lyman, F. (2003). *Think-pair-share SmartCard.* San Clemente, CA: Kagan Publishing.

Marzano, R. J., Norford, J. S., Paynter, D. E., Pickering, D. J., & Gaddy, B. B. (Eds.). (2001). *Handbook for classroom instruction that works.* Alexandria, VA: Association for Supervision and Curriculum Development.

Mendieta Jr., G. (2005). *Pictorial mathematics: An engaging visual approach to the teaching and learning of mathematics.* Etiwanda, CA: Meaningful Learning.

Mora, J. K. (1998). *The language-concept connection: Principles of sheltered English instruction.* Retrieved November 15, 2006, from http://coe.sdsu.edu/people/jmora/Lng%2DConcept/

Moschkovich, J. N. (in press). Using two languages when learning mathematics. *Educational Studies in Mathematics: Multilingual Mathematics Classrooms [Special issue].*

Moschkovich, J. N. (2002). A situated and sociocultural perspective on bilingual mathematics learners. *Mathematical Thinking and Learning, 4*(2–3), 189–212.

Moyer, P. S. (2001). Are we having fun yet? How teachers use manipulatives to teach mathematics. *Educational Studies in Mathematics: An International Journal, 47*(2), 175–197.

National Council of Teachers of Mathematics. (2000). *Principles and standards for teaching mathematics,* Reston, VA: Author.

National Research Council. (2001). *Adding it up: Helping children learn mathematics.* J. Kilpatrick, J. Swafford, & B. Findell (Eds.). Mathematics Learning Study Committee, Center for Education, Division of Behavioral and Social Sciences and Education. Washington, DC: National Academy Press.

Nelson, B. (1996). *Learning English: How school reform fosters language acquisition and development for limited English proficient elementary school students.* Santa Cruz, CA: National Center for Research on Cultural Diversity and Second Language Learning.

Newell, J. (1984). Advance organizers: Their construction and use in instructional development. (ERIC Document Reproduction Service No. ED 298908.)

O'Malley, J. M., & Valdez Pierce, L. (1996). *Authentic assessment for English language learners: Practical approaches for teachers.* New York: Addison-Wesley.

Paivio, A. (1990). *Mental representations: A dual-coding approach.* New York: Oxford University Press.

Payne, J. (Ed.). (1990). *Mathematics for the young child.* Reston, VA: National Council of Teachers of Mathematics.

PBS TeacherLine. (2002). *Developing mathematical thinking with effective questions.* Arlington, VA: Author. Retrieved November 15, 2006, from http://teacherline.pbs.org/teacherline/resources/questionsheet_vma.pdf

Risner, G. P., Nicholson, J. I., & Webb, B. (1994). *Levels of comprehension promoted by the Cooperative Integrated Reading and Composition (CIRC) Program.* Florence: University of North Alabama (ERIC Document Reproduction Service No. ED 381 751).

Rubenstein, R. N., & Thompson, D. R. (2001). Learning mathematical symbolism: Challenges and instructional strategies. *Mathematics Teacher, 94*(4), 265–271.

Schoenfeld, A. (2002). Making mathematics work for all children: Issues of standards, testing, and equity. *Educational Researcher, 31*(1), 13–25.

Shigematsu, K., & Sowder, L. (1994). Drawings for story problems: Practices in Japan and the United States. *Arithmetic Teacher, 41*(9), 544–547.

Short, D., & Echevarria, J. (2004). Teacher skills to support English language learners. *Association for Supervision and Curriculum Development,* December 2004–January 2005, 8–13.

Siegler, R. (2003). Implications of cognitive science research for mathematics education. In J. Kilpatrick, W. G. Martin, & D. Schifter (Eds.), *A research companion to principles and standards for school mathematics* (pp. 289–303). Reston, VA: National Council of Teachers of Mathematics.

Smith, S. P. (2003). Representation in school mathematics: Children's representations of problems. In J. Kilpatrick, W. G. Martin, & D. Schifter (Eds.), *A research companion to principles and standards for school mathematics* (pp. 263–274). Reston, VA: National Council of Teachers of Mathematics.

Solomon, J., & Rhodes, N. C. (1995). *Conceptualizing academic language.* Retrieved November 15, 2006, from National Center for Research on Cultural Diversity and Second Language Learning Web site: http://www.ncela.gwu.edu/pubs/ncrcdsll/rr15.htm

Sowell, E. (1989). Effects of manipulative materials in mathematics instruction. *Journal for Research in Mathematics Education, 20,* 498–505.

Spanos, G., Rhodes, N., Dale, T., & Crandall, J. (1988). Linguistic features of mathematical problem solving: Insights and applications. In R. R. Cocking & J. P. Mestre (Eds.), *Linguistic and cultural influences on mathematics learning* (pp. 221–240). Hillsdale, NJ: Erlbaum.

Sternberg, R. J., & Spear-Swerling, L. (1996). *Teaching for thinking.* Washington, DC: American Psychological Association.

Sullivan, P., & Clarke, D. (1991, October). Catering to all abilities through good questions. *Teaching Children Mathematics,* 14–18.

Teachers of English to Speakers of Other Languages (TESOL). (1997). *ESL standards for pre-K-12 students* [online ed.]. Alexandria, VA: Author. Retrieved November 15, 2006, from http://www.tesol.org/s_tesol/seccss.asp?CID=113&DID=1583

Terry, M. K. (1996). An investigation of differences in cognition when utilizing math manipulatives and math manipulative software. *Dissertation Abstracts International, 5*(07), 2650.

Thompson, P. W. (1994). Concrete materials and teaching for mathematical understanding. *Arithmetic Teacher 41*(9), 556–558.

Tse, L. (2001). *Why don't they learn English: Separating fact from fallacy in the US language debate.* New York: Teachers College Press.

Valdez, G., Svedkauskaite, A., & McNabb, M. (2002). *Critical issue: Mastering the mosaic—Framing impact factors to aid limited-English-proficient students in mathematics and science.* Retrieved November 15, 2006, from North Central Regional Educational Laboratory Web site: http://www.ncrel.org/sdrs/areas/issues/content/cntareas/math/ma700.htm

Vygotsky, L. S. (1978). *Mind in society: The development of higher psychological processes.* Cambridge, MA: Harvard University Press.

Weiss, Dana M. Freer. (2006). Keeping it real: The rationale for using manipulatives in the middle grades. *Mathematics Teaching in the Middle School, 11*(5), 238–242.

Weiss, I. R., Heck, D. J., & Shimkus, E. S. (2004, Spring). Looking inside the classroom: Mathematics teaching in the United States. *National Council of Supervisors of Mathematics Journal,* 23–32.

Weiss, I. R., Pasley, J. D., Smith, P. S., Banilower, E. R., & Heck, D. J. (2003, May). *Highlights report—Looking inside the classroom: A study of K-12 mathematics and science education in the United States.* Retrieved November 15, 2006, from http://www.horizon-research.com/reports/2003/insidetheclassroom/highlights.php

WGBH Educational Foundation. (2003). *Teaching math, grades 3–5, session 5: Representation.* Retrieved November 15, 2006, from Annenberg Media Web site: http://www.learner.org/channel/courses/teachingmath/grades3_5/session_05/index.html

Willoughby, T., Desmarias, S., Wood, E., Sims, S., & Kalra, M. (1997). Mechanisms that facilitate the effectiveness of elaboration strategies. *Journal of Educational Psychology, 89*(4), 682–685.

Wood, D., Bruner, J., & Ross, G. (1976). The role of tutoring in problem solving. *Journal of Child Psychology and Psychiatry, 17,* 89–100.

Index

Academic language
  classroom discussion
      goals, 26–27
  comprehensible input and, 97
  discussion of, 25–27
  key vocabulary introduction,
      25–26
  key word focus, 26
  language goals, 21
  math vocabulary development,
      21–22
  mathematics goals, 20–21
  opportunities to use, 22
  practice/discussion questions, 28
  primary language/cognate
      support for, 21
  research on, 27
  research rationale for, 15–16
  teaching decisions, 22–23
  teaching example, 16–20,
      17 (fig), 18 (fig)
  teaching example discussion,
      20–23
  teaching tips, 23–25
  visual aids for, 17 (fig),
      18 (fig), 23, 24 (fig)
  See also Conversational language
Advance organizer, 34, 57, 69–70
  See also Graphic organizer
Affective filter, 102
Algebraic reasoning teaching
      example, 30–35

Bar diagram, 17, 18 (fig),
      19, 69 (fig), 76 (fig), 79
Base-ten block diagram,
      61 (fig)–63 (fig), 65, 69
Basic Interpersonal Communication
      Skills (BICS), 1, 12, 27, 66
Brenner's Communication
      Framework, 13

Chart
  hundreds, 23
  place value, 51
  tally, 77 (fig), 79
  two-column, 32 (fig), 33,
      34, 37, 69–70
Choral reading/response, 23, 33
Cognates, 21
Cognitive Academic Language
      Proficiency Skills (CALPS),
      15, 66
Cognitive Academic Language
      Skills (CALS), 12
Complex Instruction Model, 13
Comprehensible input
  conceptual understanding
      and, 101
  discussion of, 99–101
  instructional strategy use
      for, 97–98, 101
  language goals, 96
  learning environment for, 96–97
  linking to prior learning, 97
  mathematics goals, 95
  maximizing comprehension
      by, 100
  monitoring student progress
      during, 101
  practice/discussion questions,
      102–103
  research on, 102
  research rationale for, 89–90
  simplified language, 100
  teaching decisions and, 96
  teaching example, 90–95
  teaching example discussion,
      95–98
  teaching tips, 98–99
Comprehensible Input
      Hypothesis, 102
Concept map, 69

Concept redundancy, 72
Concrete materials
    comprehensible input and, 97–98
    computer-based manipulative
        use, 49
    concrete-pictorial-abstract
        sequence, viability of, 51–52
    defining, 41
    discussion of, 49–52
    language goals, 47
    manipulative material use, 49,
        50–51, 52–53
    mathematics goals, 46
    multiple representation use, 47
    practice/discussion questions, 53
    preplanning key lessons, 48
    proper/improper use of, 51
    research on, 52–53
    research rationale for, 41–42
    semi-concrete representations, 51
    sensory-concrete materials,
        41–42
    teaching example, 42–46
    teaching example discussion,
        46–48
    teaching tips, 48–49
    use of, 47
    when to use, 50–51
Conversational language
    classroom climate and, 8, 10
    defining, 1
    discussion of, 9–12
    effective prompts for, 11
    equal participation,
        ensuring, 9, 11–12
    importance in learning
        mathematics, 2, 10
    language goals, 6–7
    mathematics goals, 6
    mixed language use during, 9, 10
    practice/discussion questions, 14
    problem-solving approach
        and, 10–11
    research on, 12–13
    research rationale for, 1–2
    sentence starters, 8 (fig)
    social scaffolding and, 10
    teaching example, 2–6,
        3 (fig), 5 (fig), 106
    teaching example discussion, 6–8
    teaching tips, 8–9
    thought processes development
        and, 7–8
    varying language proficiency
        levels and, 7

visual representation use, 8, 9 (fig)
    See also Academic language
Cooperative learning groups, 13
Critical thinking skills, 82–83

Diagram
    bar, 17, 18 (fig), 19, 69 (fig),
        76 (fig), 79
    base-ten block, 61 (fig)–
        63 (fig), 65, 69
    rectangular, 63 (fig), 64 (fig), 65
District fifth-grade benchmark
    teaching example, 42–48

ESL Standards for PreK-12, 13
Everyday language. *See*
    Conversational language

Front-loading vocabulary, 25

Geometric attribute teaching
    example, 2–8, 106
Graphic organizer, 68–69, 71, 72
    See also Advance organizer

Hundreds chart, 23

i + 1 teaching strategy, 102
Instructional Conversational
    Model, 13
Instructional scaffolding, 30
Integrated-concrete knowledge, 41
Internal chatter, 27

Krashen, Stephen, 102

Language functions, 27
Lesson planning map
    blank, 107–108
    example of, 109–110

Manipulative materials,
    49, 50–51, 52–53
Mathematical representation,
    defining, 52
Mathematical thinking, sample
    questions for developing,
    113–114
Mind map, 69
Mixed language use, 9, 10
Multiple representations, 47

National Council of Teachers of
    Mathematics (NCTM), 2, 30, 73
National Research Council, 30

Natural language. *See* Conversational language
Nonlinguistic representation. *See* Visual learning
Number sentence, 17–18, 19, 20, 57 (fig), 65, 82

Organizational skills, 9 (fig), 101
See also Advance organizer; Graphic organizer

Perimeter/multiplicative scaling teaching example, 90–98
Physical activity, incorporating into lesson, 99
Probability introduction teaching example, 74–80
Procedural scaffolding, 30

Question frame, 81 (fig), 83
Questioning strategies
challenging questions, 83–84
comprehensible input and, 98
critical thinking skills and, 82–83
discussion of, 81–86
fluency level effect on, 83
implications for teachers, 82
language goals, 79–80
language proficiency levels and, 84–86
mathematics goals, 79
multiple goals and, 80
practice/discussion questions, 87
question frame, 81 (fig), 83
questions/discussions among students, 80
research on, 86–87
research rationale for, 73–74
sample questions for all learners, 113–114
sentence frame, 83
Snail Race Game board for, 74–75 (fig), 111–112
teaching example, 74–79
teaching example discussion, 79–80
teaching tips, 80–81

Rectangular diagram, 63 (fig), 64 (fig), 65
Reflective talk, 27
Relational equity, 13

Scaffolding
access to lesson, 35
comprehensible input and, 97

cooperative group work as provider of, 37–38
defining, 36, 38
difference from planned direct instruction, 38–39
discussion of, 36–39
instructional, 30
language goals, 34
lesson planning map, 107–110
mathematics goals, 34
practice/discussion questions, 40
problem solving emphasis, benefit of, 38
procedural, 30
research on, 39–40
research rationale for, 29–30
routine strategy and, 39
sentence prompt for, 35
support during lesson, 35
teaching example, 30–34, 32 (fig)
teaching example discussion, 34–35
teaching tips, 35–36
using to support EL development, 39
verbal, 30
visual aids for, 32 (fig), 35, 36, 37, 39
Semi-concrete representations, 51
Sensory-concrete knowledge, 41
Sensory-concrete materials, 41–42
Sentence frame, 9, 19–20, 22, 39, 83
Sentence prompt, 35
Sentence starter, 8 (fig)
Snail Race Game board, 74–75 (fig), 111–112
Social communication. *See* Conversational language
Specially Designed Academic Instruction in English (SDAIE), 89–90
Standards, ESL Standards for PreK–12, 13
Standards for Effective Pedagogy, 99–100
Syntactic structures, mathematical, 27

t-chart. *See* Two-column chart
t-table. *See* Two-column chart
Tables, 9 (fig)
Tally chart, 77 (fig), 79
Think-Pair-Share, 9, 11

Total Physical Response (TPR), 67
Two-column chart, 32 (fig), 33,
    34, 37, 69–70
Two-digit multiplication teaching
    example, 56–67

Venn diagrams, 68 (fig), 69
Verbal representations, 47
Verbal scaffolding, 30
Visual learning
    academic language and, 17 (fig),
        18 (fig), 23, 24 (fig)
    advance organizer, 34, 57, 69–70
    auditory learning and, 70
    bar diagram/graph, 17, 18 (fig),
        19, 69 (fig), 76 (fig), 79
    base-ten block diagram, 61 (fig)–
        63 (fig), 65, 69
    charts, 9 (fig), 23, 32 (fig), 33, 34,
        37, 69–70, 77 (fig), 79
    cognitive tasks and, 66–67, 68–71
    comprehensible input and, 98
    conversational language
        and, 8, 9 (fig)
    diagrams, 17, 18 (fig), 19, 60 (fig),
        61 (fig)–63 (fig), 64 (fig), 65,
        69, 69 (fig), 76 (fig), 79
    graphic organizer, 68–69, 71, 72
    hundreds chart, 23

language goals, 65
mathematics goals, 65
number line, 23, 69–70 (fig)
number sentence, 17–18, 19,
    20, 57 (fig), 65, 82
practice/discussion
    questions, 72
rectangular diagram, 63 (fig),
    64 (fig), 65
research on, 71–72
research rationale for, 55–56
scaffolding and, 32 (fig), 35,
    36, 37, 39
tally chart, 77 (fig), 79
teaching example, 56–64
teaching example discussion,
    65–67
teaching tips, 67
two-column chart, 32 (fig), 33,
    34, 37, 69–70
uses of, 70–71
Vygotsky, L. S., 29, 38, 40

Word card, 24 (fig)
Word problem teaching
    example, 16–20
Word wall, 23, 24 (fig)

Zone of proximal development, 102

CORWIN PRESS

The Corwin Press logo—a raven striding across an open book—represents the union of courage and learning. Corwin Press is committed to improving education for all learners by publishing books and other professional development resources for those serving the field of PreK–12 education. By providing practical, hands-on materials, Corwin Press continues to carry out the promise of its motto: **"Helping Educators Do Their Work Better."**